Ultimate Oregon C Lincoln City

(Neskowin, Gleneden Beach)

Every Beach Access, Odd Facts, Fun Finds

Andre' Hagestedt, words and photos

To find lodging in Lincoln City, see
https://www.beachconnection.net/lincolncity. This also contains even more details and updated articles, the virtual tour that includes maps, as well as food / dining listings.
All contents (except OPRD photos) copyright Andre' Hagestedt.

Table of Contents

HOW TO USE THIS BOOK..5

INTRODUCTION...6

Lincoln City (Neskowin, Gleneden Beach) Quick Guide...............8

GENERAL LINCOLN CITY (AND NESKOWIN, GLENEDEN BEACH) DETAILED GUIDE..................................21

    BEACH SAFETY...21

GENERAL FEATURES, ADVICE, SECRETS, FUN FINDS.....24

    Seasons of Lincoln City..24

    Beachcombing at Lincoln City..26

    AGATES OF LINCOLN CITY.......................................31

        Odd Facts: Giant Agate Vein....................................31

    Whales..34

    Bald Eagles of Lincoln City..37

    Tidepools..38

    Do Not Feed the Birds or Wildlife...................................38

    Second Summer...40

    Early Spring of February...43

    Secret Spring..44

Unusual Sights – Rarities in General....................................48

DETAILED BEACHES AND LANDMARKS GUIDE..............52

    Neskowin..52

    History: Wild Storm Surges of Neskowin...........................54

    Mysterious Northern Sands...55

    Neskowin's Ghost Forest..57

        Are Neskowin's Ghost Forests in Danger?.....................58

        History of the Village...61

    Cascade Head and Trails..62

    Startling Geology: Cascade Head is an Extinct Volcano..........63

    Odd History: the Shipwreck and Skeleton of Three Rox Bay..68

    Corridor of Mystery..72

    Highway 18...72

        Coming from the North...73

        Otis..74

    History: Pixieland and Pixie Kitchen.................................74

    History: How Lincoln City Was Formed.............................78

    Odd History: How Lincoln City Was Named........................81

History: Site of Pixie Kitchen, Wecoma Beach (Lincoln City), Oregon..84
Devil's Lake State Recreation Area and Campground............88
   Sparky the Wish Guardian...89
Roads End State Recreational State..90
Secret Accesses: 66th St. and 7200 Block..............................93
Odd Fact: Lincoln City Hides a Second Bay...........................94
Odd Fact: Where Waves Can Go the Wrong Direction...........96
Secret Beach: NW 50th...100
Logan Road Back to Lincoln City...102
Grace Hammond Access – NW 35th...103
NW Jetty and NW Inlet...104
Access at NW 26th...105
NW 21st Access...106
Odd History: Tornado Takes Out Motel.................................107
Midtown Area – and Odd History...110
Odd History: Lincoln Statue...112
Secret Park: Oceanview Walk Park...113
NW 15th Access and Ramp..115
Hidden Beach Access Near D River..116
Inlet Court Access...117
Devils Lake State Recreational Area.......................................117
Lincoln City Cultural Center and Visitors Information Center
....117
D River Wayside..118
Odd Facts: D River Dispute Over World Record....................119
Odd Facts: D River Wayside's Changing Face........................122
Canyon Drive Beach Access..123
Lincoln City Outlets Mall...125
Agnes Creek Green Space and Trail.......................................125
Clifftop Drive Along SW Anchor..126
Nelscott District...127
Curious History: WW2 Submarine Lookout - Motel Life......128
Crazy History: Storm Damages Balcony.................................132
SW 33rd St. Access..135
SW 35th Access...136
Odd History: Joe the Sea Lion..138
History: Constructing the Inn at Spanish Head......................142

North Lincoln County Historical Museum..............................146
Overlook Park...147
Odd History: Redhead Roundup...148
Taft and Siletz Bay...149
Odd Facts: Colored Rocks at the Bend...................................150
Jennifer Sears Glass Art Studio...151
History: The Pines Hotel, The Pines Bar................................151
Siletz Bay..153
Odd History: Mysterious Shipwreck and Its Legends............156
Siletz Bay Park and the Refuge...159
Siletz River and Kernville..161
Odd Facts: Siletz Keys and Dead Trees..................................162
Josephine Young Park...163
Salishan – Salishan Spit..163
Gleneden Beach..164
Gleneden Beach State Recreation Site....................................166
Heading South...166
ABOUT ANDRE' GW HAGESTEDT.....................................168

HOW TO USE THIS BOOK

This guide to Neskowin, Lincoln City and Gleneden Beach is set up in three main parts: the Quick Guide of each beach access and attraction, general beach facts and travel advice for the area – and then a much more detailed guide to all those beaches and attractions with the full meal deal of gobs and oodles of unique information, history, oddities, secrets and more.

The detailed section you may find cumbersome if you're actually on the coast or in the middle of trip planning, and you don't want to wade through all the deeper stuff. So the beach Quick Guide will allow you to skim quickly as you're on the road, giving you a brief look at where you're going. But the true fun is in all the details, oddities, secrets and history – which you can bounce down to at any time.

Milepost markers are used whenever possible, as in "MP 22." These are the little green signs by the sides of the highway with such numbers, and they start at 0 in Astoria and get bigger as you head south. These guides also work their way from north to south. However, since most beaches in Lincoln City are far off 101, this book doesn't utilize a lot of these markers.

To find lodging in Lincoln City, Neskowin and Gleneden Beach, along with the virtual tours, restaurants and updated articles, see https://www.beachconnection.net/lincolncity. The virtual tour for Gleneden Beach is at https://www.beachconnection.net/depoebay.

For more images of these subjects, link suggestions are provided – or simply to go BeachConnection.net and do a search on that subject. Full color photos will be in great abundance there.

INTRODUCTION

The whole purpose of this book series is to show the multiple layers around you in each Oregon coast town. And the whole point of that is to provide new ways to enjoy and indulge in these beach burghs.

The thing about Lincoln City is….there's A LOT OF things about Lincoln City.

There's the obvious: Families and romancing couples will find plenty of means of repose and loafing around. The pristine beaches, the eateries, fine hotels and rentals, and the culture. The outdoorsy types will dig the agates, the hikes, the kayaking, and plenty of crabbing or clamming. Those of a more alternative culture and younger age bracket will love the freaky dive bar scene here, which can be more David Lynch than Lynch himself, then work off your hangover the next day with some exhilarating beach exploration – such as the oddball things found in this book.

Below even that multilayered surface, however, there are the wonders of nature, history and science that aren't so obvious: things that can help you appreciate what this place is all about. Sometimes knowing what it means, when it comes to a landmark or an old building, brings a more wide-eyed wonder.

Every coastal town has its history, but Lincoln City's is rather special in some ways. There are aspects particularly gritty and full of intrigue in this place's past: from its speakeasies and hookers 100 years ago, the intricate journey of the much-loved Pixieland and Pixie Kitchen, to how the town was formed from seven or eight different little communities. Plus, Lincoln City was very nearly called

Lincoln Shores or Surfland. Enough historical surprises lurk here to create yet another whole book.

Then there are the more recent historical happenings: the ways in which storms have seriously ripped up the area. Even more extraordinary: those famed and ancient ghost forests of Neskowin may be in danger.

Going back much farther in time, this place has a hellish story to tell. Its geology is rather unusual in some ways, in that one of its main features used to be a giant volcano. A gargantuan one: as much as two thousand feet high. This and other fascinating underground dynamics have real impact today: it helped create the bundle of agates you find. There's a remarkable surprise about that in this book.

Flanking it on each side is sleepy Neskowin and slightly less drowsy Gleneden Beach: you get to journey further into those gorgeous little hideouts even more.

Like the other books in this series, you'll find some parts touting the same scientific curiosities: glowing sand, weird beach creatures, green flash at sunset, etc. Still, most of those wacky features have their aspects distinctive to Lincoln City, and that's included here. Especially the whale watching action and storms: it's a different ballgame.

If you're happy with your means of kicking back on the beach, then maybe read no further. But I dare you. Even if you think you know it all about Lincoln City, well, to quote the bad '80s metal song: "You got another thing comin'."

> *- Andre' GW Hagestedt*
> *Oregon Coast Beach Connection*

Lincoln City (Neskowin, Gleneden Beach) Quick Guide

Neskowin

As you're zipping down 101 from Pacific City, at MP 98 the picturesque and mesmerizing village of Neskowin pops up, containing a handful of condos, a golf course, perhaps two or three businesses and a bundle of charming homes.

Neskowin's Ghost Forest

This downright spectacular oddity is almost a rare sight along the Oregon coast, and you may not know just how spectacular it is unless you know what you're looking at. They are about two thousand years old. You have to cross the often-swift creek to get to it: it lies just beyond Proposal Rock.

Mysterious Northern Sands

Northern Neskowin could well be the magnificent treasure of the tiny town. Head north on Breakers Avenue and you start encountering westbound streets along the beachfront with the names of other Oregon towns. The final access at Corvallis Avenue is stunning.

Cascade Head and Trails

Take Three Rocks Road to one of the major trailheads for Cascade Head, or find some along that "corridor of mystery" where the road winds and turns beneath thick forestland.

The most used trail is the Conservancy's 2.7-mile path, which takes you to some seriously gorgeous bluffs. That one's a 3.4-mile roundtrip from the lower trailhead, which you'll find along Savage Road, off Three Rocks Road.

The upper trailhead is much easier, although it's not open all year: only a two-mile roundtrip, accessible from Cascade Head Road, near MP 101, in Tillamook County.

The Hart's Cove Trail, also closed from January to May, is accessible by Cascade Head Road.

Cascade Head was once a volcano. Three Rox Bay also contains some strange history regarding the skeleton of a giant and a shipwreck. See the full guide for these.

Corridor of Mystery

That stretch between Neskowin and the Highway 18 junction that whizzes past Cascade Head has been sometimes referred to as the "Corridor of Mystery" by some locals and regular visitors, because of its thick canopy of trees and a sense of the impenetrable all around you. This section also includes markers for the 45th Parallel, which is the point halfway between the equator and the north pole.

Highway 18

Along Highway 18, outside Portland, you'll encounter the lush Yamhill wine country and quaint towns like Dundee. There's also charming McMinnville, with Howard Hughes' Spruce Goose in a museum, an interesting arts community, some fine culinary pleasures and a quaint old downtown area. At Grande Ronde, near the casino, Highway 22 from Salem meets up with Highway 18 and heads through the lush forestland of the Van Duzer Corridor until it wanders past Otis and enters Lincoln City.

Otis

You'll encounter this tiny town just a few miles before reaching Lincoln City. It's famous for the legendary breakfasts of the Otis Café.

Pixieland

On Highway 101, not far from the Highway 18 junction, you'll find a plaque showing where Pixieland was. If you blink, you'll miss it. The whole tale actually begins with Pixie Kitchen (see the full chapters later).

Devil's Lake State Recreation Area and Campground

Head south onto East Devil's Lake Rd. to reach this favorite camping, fishing and boating spot. There are 50 tent sites, 10 yurt spots, a great number of electrical and full hook-up sites that can even have cable TV, paved parking and a load of other amenities in the campground. There's also a hiker/biker camp. This is the northern access to the lake. oregonstateparks.org or (800) 551-6949.

Sparky the Wish Guardian

The Devil's Lake Creature in Lincoln City – a massive metallic creature also known as "Sparky the Wish Guardian" – was put into place here back in 2013. The whimsical sculpture sits above Devils Lake at Regatta Grounds Park, residing at the entrance.

Site of Pixie Kitchen, Wecoma Beach (Lincoln City), Oregon

Between NW 36th St. and NW 35th St., next to the big credit union building, is where the famed Pixie Kitchen was. Now, it's a coffee stand surrounded by a parking lot and pavement.

Roads End State Recreational State

This is where the town simply stops, butting up against a headland called Roads End Point that seems to slightly echo the shape of Cascade Head just beyond it and the prominent God's Thumb formation in the distance. This is the last public beach access before you have to drive 15 or so miles north to hit the Three Rocks Road area. Many of the town's real surprises lie at Roads End, such as the cave and piercing Wizard Rock – all a bit of a hike from the main access.

Secret Accesses: 66th St. and 7200 Block

Just beyond the main park, up Logan Road, two more secret accesses grant you passage to the sands. They're tiny and they're extremely difficult to find. One, without any parking, is simply a path between homes around 66th St.

The other is marked as a day use spot around the 7200 block of Logan Road, and it features maybe two parking spots on the concrete. Both are about a quarter mile north of the main parking lot, so you're cutting a little out of your strenuous hike to the end of the beach and its secrets – but not much.

Odd Fact: Lincoln City Hides a Second Bay

There is what could be termed yet a second bay in this central Oregon coast resort town: almost another little cozy cove, aside from the more well-known and even famous Siletz Bay at the southern side. Very loosely speaking, it's a kind of a cove, and not something even officially recognized by the city or visitors bureau. But it is a fun and funky little geographic delight you've likely never noticed before, and yet it's very real. More at the full guide.

Secret Beach: NW 50th

This one, at around NW 50th St., is about the closest you can get to a secret beach in this busy town.

At the very northern end of town, along Logan Road and between the casino and Roads End State Recreational Site, look for the sign pointing to NW 50th amid the placid neighborhoods.

Logan Road Back to Lincoln City

To get back to other beach accesses you have to continue south on Logan Road. Just off Logan, before the massive intersection and the strip mall, is the entrance to the Chinook Winds Casino complex. Find NW 40th there and you'll discover a tiny public beach access at its end. There's plenty of parking and decent restroom facilities.

Beach Accesses off Jetty Ave. and the Semi Secret Road

At the casino, you have the option to zip back up to Highway 101 or continue on NW 40th around a tiny curve and a road that narrows enough it's barely able to hold two lanes. This leads onto Jetty Avenue and a whole host of fun beach accesses. It's quicker than driving back up to Logan, onto 101 and then down one of the side streets again.

Grace Hammond Access – NW 35th

Found more or less at the bottom of NW 34th, if you take that road straight westward from the highway. There's a small parking lot, a little viewpoint with a picnic table, restroom facilities and a wheelchair-accessible ramp down to this broad, sandy beach.

It's technically part of NW 35th Place, but it's known by the name Grace Hammond, after the woman who donated the land to the state decades ago. One of the more obvious features is the memorial to deceased dogs, a simple sign showing the names of much-loved mutts who have passed on.

NW Jetty and NW Inlet

You generally won't find any beach accesses here as it's all cliffs. The hotels lining the cliffs have their own private beach entryways, however. Suddenly, at NW 26th and NW Jetty, NW Inlet becomes the westernmost drive along the cliffs, starting with a rather stunning beach access.

Access at NW 26th

A small but decently-sized parking lot is surrounded by an atmospheric wall made of large stones, coming complete with bike racks. It gives the place a slight medieval castle vibe. You'll find restrooms here and a picnic table.

There are some concrete steps down to the beach – well, a lot of steps. One of the fascinating features is the remnants of another stony stairway which apparently was destroyed in recent decades.

NW 21st Access

You won't find much parking – maybe four or five spots, max. The centerpiece is that long, long....extremely long staircase. Parking is limited as it's squeezed between two parts of the hotel complex.

Midtown Area

Here's one moniker that simply came from modern times and not one of the tiny communities that created the whole of Lincoln City. Midtown is that area from about NW 19th down close to about NW 10th or so, which includes a whole host of businesses both historic and recent. Everything from books, ice cream, taffy, gourmet food, clothing to wacky dive bars for the nocturnally adventurous sit along here.

Lincoln Statue

It sits on NE 22nd St., just a block or two off Highway 101: a simple depiction of a young Abe Lincoln on his horse, reading a book.

Secret Park: Oceanview Walk Park

If you blink you'll miss it. Look for NW 16th street, in the midtown area, then head towards the ocean. This one is a simple and quaint collection of sidewalk and bench overlooking the waves and sand. It's tiny but it's lovely. There are no beach accesses between NW 21st and NW 15th, but they're not far apart. There is only the viewpoint here above it all.

NW 15th Access and Ramp

One of the few places on the entire Oregon coast where you can drive your car is here, but within a small, restricted area. It's also about the only major tidepool spot in Lincoln City. Restrooms, benches and a stairway as well. From here, NW Harbor winds and turns through motel territory but dead-ends and produces no beach accesses. Head back up to NW Inlet to continue on the back roads here.

Hidden Beach Access Near D River

You'll find this one about two blocks north of the D River and Kyllo's Restaurant, along Inlet Ave. It's tucked between two of the motels here. The pathway itself may be a secret but the nearby accesses of the D River assures that there's a lot of people here. It's technically at the end of NW 5th St. but there is no street sign.

Inlet Court Access

Just the other side of the river (or stream), on the northern face of the big restaurant at the D River, sits another tiny access that gets you onto the northern section of the D River access.

Devils Lake State Recreational Area

Head east at the traffic light at NE 6th St. to reach this favorite camping, fishing and boating spot. There are heaps of tent sites, yurt spots, paved parking and a load of other amenities in the campground. See the previous full listing.

Lincoln City Cultural Center and Visitors Information Center

If you're not looking up everything digitally, or need a real person to talk to, the info center is the place. Also includes the Lincoln City Cultural Center and its gallery, as well as the farmer's / crafter's market. 540 NE Hwy 101, Lincoln City, Oregon. 541-994-9994. https://www.lincolncity-culturalcenter.org/.

More on the visitors center at https://www.oregoncoast.org.

D River Wayside

A big parking lot with all the facilities, viewing platforms and a sometimes-wild surf greet you here. In between, there's tons of sand and a creek for recreation. Sometimes, the city places volleyball nets on the sand so you can get your game on.

It can also be a great spot for gravel beds – and thus agates – even in summer.

Canyon Drive Beach Access

It's the only gap in a mile or so radius of cliffs and neighborhoods. Take SW 11th from the main stretch of Highway 101 in Lincoln City until it dead-ends at this cozy beach entrance. A restroom area and a handful of parking spots is what you see at first, but it's actually part beach and part lakeside park.

Lincoln City Outlets Mall

A massive shoppers' paradise by any standards, but if you're not into dealing with the throngs – at any time of year – then stick to the beaches. It's found on Highway 101 near SW 12 St. Really, you can't miss it. (541) 996-5000.

Agnes Creek Green Space and Trail

If you're on Highway 101, or you've just begun to go south on SW Coast Ave., you'll see a lot of trees for a good mile or two. This is a forest within a coastal resort town, with lots of forested hiking trails. It's unbroken except by SW Bard Rd, which meets up with SW Coast Ave. from Highway 101 just south of SW 17th St., via a long, winding and twisting – and purely gravel - road.

Clifftop Drive Along SW Anchor

Along SW Coast, there are no public beach accesses. Some resort hotels and rental homes have their own switchbacking stairways down the cliff, however. It eventually turns into SW Anchor.

There is, however, a stunning but simple gravel pullout or two where you can gaze out over the cliffs and down to the beach below.

Nelscott District

The first beach access you'll encounter (a mile south of the Canyon Drive access) is SW 33rd Ave. Anything north of that is either clifftop homes (or along Highway 101 you're on the eastern face of the forest lands of the Agnes Creek Open Space). The old Nelscott district is a charming and comely little place, lying just north of the enormous Inn at Spanish Head, including a large bluff that's been turned into a winding street full of beautiful homes.

SW 33rd St. Access

Head down SW 32nd or SW 35th to find this. A tiny, nondescript access with minimal parking, a water fountain and a handicapped-accessible ramp doesn't seem like much at first glance. This place is the key to a couple of astounding things: some great wave action in winter and the closest access to some large bulbous rock formations that help fuel the fun finds of agates in Lincoln City.

SW 35th Access

Take a turn west on SW 32nd St. and you'll find it just to the north, or simply head down SW 35th St. A tiny parking lot with restrooms and a small set of steps down to the cushy, thick sand, this is where the tideline can get quite steep and result in raucous waves that crash in hard and fast, but then dissipate into timid little lines of white foam.

North Lincoln County Historical Museum

Everything you ever wanted to know about Lincoln City's past, including artifacts from local native tribes, pioneers and old photos as well as a collection of glass floats. It also hosts numerous lectures and events that are particularly interesting.

4907 US-101. (541) 996-6614.
www.northlincolncountyhistoricalmuseum.org/

Overlook Park

It sits at the end of a suburban street (namely Beach Ave.), featuring this incredible viewpoint of Siletz Bay and a bench at the edge of this cliff.

Taft and Siletz Bay

Taft is a charming little place to go wandering – either on the beach or along the business district. A funky-colored surf shop sits nearby, as well as coffee shops, pizza joints, gourmet hamburgers and some delicious ethnic surprises. It's yummy and generally quite creative.

Take the boardwalk out onto the bay, and maybe watch seals watching you.

Jennifer Sears Glass Art Studio

Appointments are necessary to make your own glass float – watching is free and no appointment required. Otherwise known as the Lincoln City Glass Center, it was originally named after Jennifer Sears 4821 SW Hwy 101. Lincoln City, Oregon. 541-996-2569. https://www.lincolncityglasscenter.com/

History: The Pines Hotel, The Pines Bar

These days, there's only a parking lot there in Taft, though you'll still see a sign declaring The Pines Restaurant and Lounge. Almost directly across the street from the bar called Snug Harbor, you'll see only concrete. Yet a decade ago there was a wild 'n crazy bar called The Pines, and before that a famed hotel.

Siletz Bay

All this is accessible by SW 51st St., just before you leave Lincoln City, if you're heading southward.

It's here where they hold the famed sandcastle festival every year, and it's here you'll find by far the most driftwood in town, perhaps on all of the Oregon coast (except for maybe one part of Rockaway Beach). Chunks of formerly floating wood are crammed together here in a way they are nowhere else on these shores. It can actually be a little difficult to move.

Siletz Bay Park and the Refuge

Look for it just a tiny bit south of the 51st Ave entrance to Siletz Bay.

This small parking lot – and another viewing area next to it – both look out over the Siletz Bay. Information kiosks and other facilities are found here, and just a short walk away sits the big pier jutting out into the bay. It's an engaging spot for a picnic and there are restrooms.

Next up: you're now entering the Siletz Bay National Wildlife Refuge, and a host of interesting features no one knows about. Access road is Millport Slough Lane on the eastern side of the highway.

Alder Island is one small section you can walk around on, and lucky for you there's the recently-installed Alder Island Nature Trail. It's a shorty, but a goodie. https://www.fws.gov/refuge/siletz_bay/. 541-867-4550.

Siletz River and Kernville

The Siletz River is the sizable body of water that feeds into the bay, meandering through the marshes, forests and hills for tens of miles. Close to the junction is teeny, tiny Kernville, surprisingly the first community developed here in the 1800s. See full guide for historical trivia.

Odd Facts: Siletz Keys and Dead Trees

Two quirky features of the area lurk around here as well. One is a vague remnant of a failed community development and the other a slightly spooky sight. See full guide.

Josephine Young Park

This is one seriously hidden park, tucked away behind a neighborhood that's tucked away behind Highway 101. Take SW 62nd westward and look for the signs leading to the park. This little wayside overlooks mostly mudflats of the Siletz Bay, but parts of it are traversable. There's some dunes along the shore as well, plus picnic spots for the hungry.

Salishan – Salishan Spit

A favorite hiking spot for many and an upscale business complex are the two high-profile facets of the Salishan district. If you're a hotel guest or a resident of the gated community, you have access to the beach from here. Otherwise, the northernmost beach access that allows you to hike the spit is down in Gleneden Beach a ways. Hiking Salishan is about an eight-mile round trip.

Gleneden Beach

These are a curious set of beaches, too. Often, there's a rather steep slope to the tide line, which causes the waves to come in hard and noisy then stop quite quickly. It's a bit freaky at first. It feels like it's going to be dangerous, but it's not.

The back road of Gleneden Beach Loop extends about a mile behind Highway 101, with junctions to 101 at either end. The southernmost end lies at the entrance to the State Park.

Secret beach accesses found by going west on Sijota St. until you reach Neptune St. Another small access sits a few streets south near Easy St. Yes, that's its real name.

Gleneden Beach State Recreation Site

There are paved paths to the beach, a lovely lookout area above and a big parking lot – plus many civilized amenities like restrooms. It's near MP 122.

GENERAL LINCOLN CITY (AND NESKOWIN, GLENEDEN BEACH) DETAILED GUIDE

BEACH SAFETY

Winter storms and sneaker waves are the most prominent danger you have to worry about in the Lincoln City area, and most beaches here are small enough to be prone to serious tidal hazards.

Always keep your eye on the tides: don't turn your back to the ocean. Stay clear of any logs in the surf: these can move easily and crush you. Stay off cliff edges when it's been raining for awhile as these can give way beneath you. Luckily, most viewpoints on any cliffs in Lincoln City are made of concrete and it's extremely difficult to stand on an unsupported spot or even find one. However, just south of town, at Gleneden Beach, there are plenty of little clifftop nook 'n crannies that you should keep clear of in rainy situations.

Special Warnings About Lincoln City: Most of the beaches are fairly small and there's little room between you and the tideline if seas are raging. Much of the time, there's either a seawall, rip rap or a cliff behind you, and the closest access point could be yards away. Not enough time for you to run out of the way of major waves. Gleneden Beach is even harsher. A few people have died there thinking they were just taking a leisurely stroll on the beach while stormwatching.

Watching of storms in Lincoln City should be done from the parking lots of larger accesses to maybe even viewpoints like the top of NW 26th, Overview Park, etc. Even then, in really massive wave events, the lower accesses and lots are not safe. Even the D River access has been known to be the recipient of giant logs getting flung onto the concrete when the wave warnings issued by officials reach the 30-foot point.

If you see a parking lot is closed off by city officials, heed that. People have been hurt by ignoring those warnings, usually from being knocked over by waves, and cars have been known to get swamped and ruined by salt water. One case in Garibaldi in the early 2000's saw a few cars actually floated for a time by a massive wave inundation, essentially considered totaled by the rush of salt water into components. The owners had ignored a closure sign.

General Warnings. During storms, you're not even really dealing with sneaker waves at this point: these are giant waves you should be staying away from, period.

One hidden danger in summertime that does not get talked about is the proliferation of sudden drops that can lurk in the tideline, ones you can't see. When summer sand levels get high enough, they can leave gigantic piles on the beaches, making interesting but enormous patterns. However, this can happen at the tideline, just beneath the waves. The problem is you can't see them, and there are large spaces between them under those waves.

If you're walking on one of these sandbars they can suddenly drop three feet to as much as ten feet. This leaves your body shocked by the fall and you may be underwater as well. You won't be able to breath. It's not as common a hazard as sneaker waves but deaths because of this do occur.

See www.BeachConnection.net for the full spectrum of safety hazards, including swimming, tidepooling and more.

GENERAL FEATURES, ADVICE, SECRETS, FUN FINDS

Seasons of Lincoln City

The whole year round, Lincoln City is hopping. Sometimes more than others. But compared to other towns, it's livelier than most whatever the season. Sure, the hotels empty out in winter and great deals are there to coax people in, but by and large this sprawling seven miles of beachy wonders has more traffic and people than most.

Lincoln City finds a way to entertain each and every season. Winter is supposed to be the dead time of the year, but big name acts at the casino, the Finders Keepers glass floats promotion, concerts and lectures at places like the Lincoln City Cultural Center or various churches, plus a vibrant live music scene at the bars keep the whole joint a jumpin'. A year-round farmers market also helps.

The glass float drops are definitely the highlight for many, which starts in September and runs all the way through Memorial Weekend in May. Sometimes storms interrupt this, but fairly rarely.

The whole year, the Culinary Center offers up fun ways of making a delicious mess, teaching you to cook a variety of scrumptious things. The North Lincoln County History proves endless historical amusement as well, including lots on the famed Pixieland and Pixie Kitchen.

Lincoln City is also known for its engaging nature walks and workshops, like those for agate hunting, crabbing, clamming, birding and much more. These are staggered throughout the year, depending on what's the hottest activity at the time.

Sometime between October and March, the town's most intriguing event pops up on just a few days notice: the Nelscott Reef Big Wave Classic. There's some gnarly waves out there, about a mile out – discovered in the early 2000s. And when conditions are right, the surfing event is called into existence. https://nelscottreef.com/.

Winter means some special caution on these beaches (as outlined in the safety chapter): the beaches are small and thus more dangerous than many during stormy conditions. Gleneden Beach is even more dangerous. Stormwatching is adequate: it's still pretty good from safer parking lots, high vantage points or your hotel room. But it's not nearly as dramatic as down south at Depoe Bay and the rocky areas surrounding it, where those basalt shelves are prime targets for whopper waves. That little town also has the spouting horn there, where spectacular wave action makes for a giant spout of sea water. It's worth the 20-minute drive from Lincoln City alone.

Agates are a huge attraction here – even in times of the year other than winter. There's a whole section on that in this book. Whales are also stellar in this area (see that chapter).

In spring and summer, kites and sand castles rule the months, along with a huge variety of other special events that feature anything from hot rods to beer. There's even a Pixie Fest that brings back to life the much-loved attraction. Fourth of July really crams the crowds into the area. Like any coastal town, make sure you make your Independence Day lodging reservations at least a month ahead of time. Most hotels and rental agencies are actually booked up by even a month away, so make an effort to get that done even earlier.

Dealing with traffic is always going to be an issue here, but it's better than the days 20 years ago when the visitors bureau actually suggested you not make left turns. During really bad traffic jams, you can sometimes skirt the northern half of 101 through town by taking the road around Devil's Lake, which starts at the northern outskirts of town and comes out again near the D River. But this isn't always possible, and it's just less frustrating by a matter of degrees.

More, deeper seasonal information in the coming chapters.

Beachcombing at Lincoln City

Velella velella (purple sailors) – photo courtesy Tiffany Boothe, Seaside Aquarium

In many ways, Lincoln City is no different for beachcombing than most sections of the Oregon coast. These long, sandy stretches yield the same funky items found from Warrenton to the California border.

There's a separate section here for agates: this addresses the wacky nature stuff that makes its way to the beaches.

The best oceanic goodies and oddities wash up in winter, fall and spring, just after storms. But summer features a few choice discoveries as well. Velella velella (those purple creatures that start to stink) tend to show up in early summer, sometimes scattered throughout the year. Also, pyrosomes have been making themselves at home – and a bit of a nuisance – in recent years, and no one knows why. More on those below. For even more information on this and more full color photos, see www.beachconnection.net.

For wilder oceanic fun, look for:

Whale Burps. These are puzzling objects that look out of place on the beach: they resemble small stacks of hay, or sometimes they show up as balls of grassy stuff. In fact, they are bundles of beach grass or sea plants from the deep that have compacted so much that they're practically rock hard. This photo was taken in Lincoln City.

Ocean Burps. The largest, broadest class of stuff you'll discover is called an "ocean burp." It really refers to a large potpourri of things – and it's different every time. There are a few items found in it more often than not, but mostly what makes this jumble of stuff connected is the fact it often shows up as a monumental, brownish pile of little bits.

It fairly frequently involves living specimens like live eggs from various species, a vast array of shells, carcasses of formerly living sea creatures, bits of wood, and so much, much more. See more at www.beachconnection.net on this.

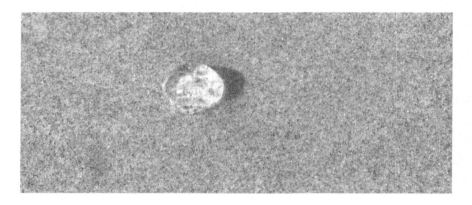

Sea Gooseberries. If some of the bubbles on the beach look a little out of place, you may have just found one. They are called comb jellies or sea gooseberries at times. You can take your pick. What you'll find is something that looks like an extra bubble from the sea foam, perhaps about the size of a dime or a quarter. But it's static, unmoving and doesn't disappear like other bits of sea foam.

The sea gooseberry has two tentacles, which are about three times longer than the body of the critter. These are lined with colloblasts – a specialized adhesive cell that helps snag food for the comb jelly.

They only live about four to six months. They're unremarkable on land, but if you come across one still living and get it into a tank of sea water, it's a gloriously beautiful, graceful but alien creature. Their many cilia refract the light, producing rainbow-like colors that can give the impression they're glowing.

Japanese Glass Floats. They're extremely rare, but it happens. Glass floats were for decades a steady and yet treasured find along the coast, but they largely disappeared in the '80s. A little known fact, however, is that January through March conditions are good for these to show up again. 2010 was actually an exceptional year for this. You've got to have patience and check the foredunes and beach grass carefully.

Lincoln City, of course, is known for its Finders Keepers event every fall through spring, where artisan-designed glass floats are dropped all over.

Creatures on a Rope or Other Objects. When manmade objects spend a decent amount of time floating on or under the water, they usually acquire some kind of life form, which then remains on it if the chunk of flotsam winds up onshore. Sometimes, it's still alive.

Lancetfish. They look like a barracuda, and they are definitely somewhat rare (or certainly sporadic). It's actually called a Longnose Lancetfish (Alepisaurus ferox), and they live as far down as 6,000 feet below the surface. Reaching up to six feet in length, most that are found on the Oregon coast are three or four feet long. Even though they are common off these waters, they live so deep it's considered an unusual event when one washes up.

Weird pyrosomes on the Oregon coast, photo courtesy Seaside Aquarium / Tiffany Boothe

Pyrosomes. This is a bizarre creature that has suddenly started washing up along the Oregon coast in recent years. It's called a pyrosome, and the ones found here are less than a foot. They are actually massive colonies of cloned creatures all connected together – and slightly related to a kind of jellyfish called a salp.

Gobs of Bull Kelp. One of the more impressive but puzzling sights are giant piles of snake-like creatures of green or brown. These are bull kelp, and each individual can be several feet to twenty feet long. They exist in sizable kelp forests off the shoreline. You can see many of them from rocky shelf areas like those around Depoe Bay and Cape Foulweather, with their little brown heads bobbing in the ocean. For this reason they often get mistaken for seals.

AGATES OF LINCOLN CITY

What happens with agates and similar rockhounding endeavors here is rather extraordinary. There are some truly amazing finds and features along these beaches. Agate hunting in Lincoln City seems to miraculously happen all year. Gravel beds open up all the time, then of course they disappear sometimes within days or even hours.

Odd Facts: Giant Agate Vein

There's a hidden agate factory beneath the sands of this central Oregon coast town. Indeed it's all over the Lincoln

City area, extending from the nearshore forests to the ocean just offshore, churning out gobs of the little colored nuggets that people love to collect so much.

The difference is in Lincoln City you can spot some of the action taking place, or at least the source.

Laura Joki runs Rock Your World gem shop in Lincoln City, a sort of eclectic place of anything to do with gems, rocks and jewelry made from such things, as well as other earthbound esoterica. In fact, she leads agate-hunting clinics in Lincoln City during some parts of the year, taking members of the public out on guided walks filled with facts.

A major feature of these tours is taking a look at two of the jasper veins visible in Lincoln City. One of the big ones is out in the open a little more often than the other. Usually, however, both aren't visible unless sand levels get below a certain level, allowing you to peek down lower and closer to the bedrock that holds all that lovely sand you're used to dipping your toes in.

The two geological wonders lurk far up into the Nelscott district, at a section where there's only cliffs and no beach accesses. It winds up rather remote, so you have to walk a ways from the SW 33rd beach access. Both are an eruption of some kind left over from millions and millions of years ago.

One is a dike eruption, meaning it was a layer of magma (or molten lava) that filled into a crack or weak spot in surrounding rock. Then some change left part or all of it exposed. The other is a dome eruption, meaning it was a large mass of lava bubbling up from the open Earth all on its own.

The dike eruption spot is the more often visible example.

"I can take people to this big eruption and you can actually walk around, and as you walk around you can actually see agates growing in the vessels or bubbles in this eruption on the beach," Joki said. "I can say: This here is where the gemstones are coming from and why."

They aren't the only sources of jasper along this beach. Joki said she's spotted them in the tidepooling areas around this part of the central Oregon coast. There's apparently one sometimes visible just beneath the water near Siletz Bay. The sources that shed these gems are located all over the beaches of Lincoln City, some parts of the inland areas and just offshore well beneath the waves.

Exactly how these veins of jasper get created is a bit complex, but it comes down to a fairly simple formula of clay, hot geyser water (or undersea water heated by eruptions) and magma with a heavy silica content, all combining to create jasper.

That kind of magma is actually called rhyolite.

"Silica plus mud equals jasper," Joki said, simplifying it further.

The dome eruption spot and the dike magma spot have some different qualities.

"Rhyolite magma has broken through the old sea floor, which is now land, what we're standing on today, and it erupted out of that sea floor," she said. "And with the hydro thermal waters that come up along its side, the dike eruption transported jasper up the side. With the dome eruption 25 yards to the north, it actually has its jasper down the middle of it, more of a throat-like water-based eruption, where it flowed through like a geyser."

The dike spot looks mostly like a giant black blob in the sand with some discolorations to it, if you look closer. But in reality it's the spot of a full-on eruption and its exact age is unknown.

All this was underwater at several points in time, but when this eruption happened it was in a period of uplift.

This bedrock that all of the Oregon coast from Yachats to Astoria sits on is called the Astoria formation. It's a form of mudstone, which came into being about 18 million years ago. It's also possible these globs of agate-producing frozen magma predate this area by tens of millions of years.

Therein lies an interesting tale.

The dome spot, Joki said, stands 12 feet from the mudstone to its top.

"I have a pic of it scoured down to the mudstone," she said. "Because it's silica rich, and silica is harder than steel, it created mudstone harder than the other mudstone around it."

Joki said the dome is visible some summers, but not always. In 2017 it wasn't; in 2018 it was. The dike eruption section is only visible when sand levels drop enough in winter.

Whales

Much of Lincoln County is blessed with a good deal of whale action, though Lincoln City is at the northern edges of this activity and thus can see just a little less of it. It's largely because of the great number of so-called resident gray whales that like to linger off the rocky reefs of the Depoe Bay area, rather than just moving on with the migrations.

Also, the area gets a good dose of Orcas now and then.

There are always a rotating population of these whales that just hang out here, which is actually called the Pacific Feeding Group by scientists. Estimates are that out of the 200,000 whales that migrate from Mexico to the waters near Alaska, about one percent – some 200 gray whales – stick around the waters from northern California up to British Columbia.

In and around Lincoln County, it's the food-rich reefs that keep more of them in the area. Along this stretch, there are plenty of eyes keeping watch on the whale numbers and reporting in, as well as outfits geared towards helping you see more. In Depoe Bay, there's the Whale Watch Center run by Oregon Parks and Recreation Department, and there and in Newport there are either plenty of whale cruise operations or scientists that study them pretty closely. Meanwhile, plenty of anecdotal whale reports come from Yachats and Lincoln City as well.

Of that 200, there are always some numbers of gray whales in Lincoln County. Something like 50 different individuals return over and over – identified and even named by people like Carrie Newell, who runs a whale cruise out of Depoe Bay and is a well-renowned author on the subject.

The big reason for this lingering about is the mycid shrimp that is a favorite food of the gray whales. Mycid shrimp like to hide in kelp forests, and there is plenty of kelp in this section of the coast, especially around rocky reef areas like Depoe Bay and Yachats. At the very least, this brings them closer to shore, though most whale sightings are actually around a mile away.

One of the key components to spotting whales is high vantage points, which Lincoln City has plenty of. It also takes plenty of patience: they take a while to show up. And many, many times they don't appear at all. Don't bother with the entitled attitude of "We saw no whales and we're bitterly disappointed," then worse yet leaving that complaint in an online review. It's nature. Get over it.

For a better chance of catching them, drive down to Depoe Bay or Newport and hop aboard one of the whale tours. You greatly increase your chances of seeing them by just heading farther out to sea. The sighting rate of these tours is pretty high when the weather is cooperating.

There's almost always a rush of Orcas in the spring, usually running from about April into May, but recent years seem to have them show up a little sooner. These are a puzzling group of transient killer whales scientists know little about. They have a longer, more beak-like appearance. What is known is that they're here to chase the newborn gray whale calves that are migrating through with their mamas.

This creates a major spectacle sometimes as a killer whale is seen living up to its name by devouring a young gray whale in front of beachgoers, or maybe a seal or sea lion. It's gruesome but fascinating. That's a rare sight, but a little less rare – but not by much – is catching sight of the Orcas in hunting mode and chasing down something at high speed.

The Whale Watch Center in Depoe Bay notes that gray whales seem to know when the killer whales are in the area. Periodically, all the grays will abruptly disappear from the center's view, and after awhile – sure enough – some Orcas come plodding through the waters.

Bald Eagles of Lincoln City

Bald eagles are spotted in all sorts of places along the Oregon coast, from the top of Oregon down to Brookings on the California border. They are certainly fairly frequent visitors in Lincoln City as well.

When to see them? Anytime of the year is equally good, according to nature expert Range Bayer, out of Newport. "We have a lot of resident adult bald eagles year-round along the Oregon coast," he said.

Bayer offered some tips for increasing your chances of spotting bald eagles. He said bays along the coast will help, like Alsea Bay at Waldport, Siletz Bay at Lincoln City, Netarts Bay at Oceanside, Florence's Siuslaw Bay, etc.

At the tideline is also a bit of a haunt for them, but given the close proximity to a lot of people that may be harder.

"Heading out on an outgoing tide is good," Bayer said. "You'll find them perched on pilings or logs. Looking up at the treelines of bays will help if you're trying to find adults."

Bayer said they're looking for fish and sometimes other birds.

Pauline Baker, with the North Coast Wildlife Rehabilitation Center near Astoria, said they are most active in the mornings and then at dusk – especially interested in low tides. Bald eagles are opportunistic hunters, seeking out stranded fish and other tidbits that low tides leave behind.

Cape Meares, near Oceanside, is known for some spectacular sights as they try and attack nests of other birds along the cliffs. This is nearly an hour's drive north of Lincoln City.

Tidepools

There are not a huge array of tidepools in the Lincoln City area, not like a few miles down the road in and around Depoe Bay or the southern end of Lincoln Beach. But they're sizable enough for plenty of critter-viewing fun. The most copious amount that is easily accessible is at the SW 15th St. ramp access, where a handful of rocky blobs contain a good number of colorful lifeforms. Another small chunk sits sometimes at the NW 40th access by the casino, depending on conditions. Often these are underwater and not accessible, however.

The largest number of colonies is at the very northern tip of Roads End where the town's beaches stop, but this is a bit remote for many casual walkers, and parts of it are fairly hazardous under most conditions anyway.

Do Not Feed the Birds or Wildlife

Yes, this is a sad thing to say and it's going to be a bummer to read. But you should not feed birds or wildlife – especially seagulls. The short of it: eating our food scraps harms them, and it makes them less frightened of humans and cars, thus endangering them even more. The other problem is that when they mass together on beaches their droppings affect water quality.

Feeding seagulls is now becoming greatly discouraged along the Oregon coast by state and local officials at a variety of levels. Cannon Beach is increasingly at the forefront of that. Various civic authorities are starting to get the word out on a wider basis, especially in towns where water quality gets affected by large flocks of birds plopping poop everywhere. Luckily, Lincoln City doesn't get hit by this too much, but most of the area is not monitored by DEQ in the first place.

Feeding seagulls is not illegal, but it is highly discouraged - and it may become illegal down the road.

To begin with, human food is bad for them. Especially the stuff that gets thrown at them more often like bread, French fries, potato chips, pizza and lunch meat. These foods have absolutely no nutritional value for gulls and can actually harm them.

Then there are the numerous traffic issues. They no longer fear cars and start to view them as big vending machines. Being highly intelligent birds they learn quickly. This is why they often don't move when you're driving through beach access parking lots.

Some fast food parking lots in particular are problematic, such as way up north in Seaside. They swarm in huge numbers there. All it takes is one French fry and you've suddenly acquired 50 birds.

Not only do the birds cause a major nuisance in terms of droppings on pavement and sheer numbers, but they get hit by other cars in the parking lot, or worse yet they wander nonchalantly into traffic on 101 and get hit there.

All hit or injured seagulls need to be euthanized. They can't be rescued or rehabilitated.

Then there are the public health issues that are the result of big flocks of seagulls. Their fecal matter gets into storm drains and hits the beach in unpleasantly large amounts. Some towns, like Cannon Beach, have had more problems with this than others. Consequently, lodgings and businesses there have been much more proactive about getting the word out to guests to "not feed the seagulls." Many lodgings in Lincoln City will declare a ban on feeding them from their patios or balconies because of the inevitable mess it leaves.

This lack of fear of vehicles has created another level of crime and vandalism as well. It gives some people more excuses to do bad things. For a time in the early 2010's, there had been numerous high profile news stories of motorists driving on beaches and killing as many as 50 seagulls at once – on purpose.

That is a crime punishable by law.

Second Summer

They call it the "second summer" on Oregon's coast and around Lincoln City, and it's really the best time of year to hit the area for a number of reasons. There's a nice combo of weather factors that come together, providing the warmest, calmest conditions of the whole year. But you'll also find lodging prices starting to dip, less people on the roads, more beaches to yourself and often no wait times at your favorite eateries.

Less people on Lincoln City's roads is a bit relative, however: there's almost always a fair amount of traffic through town.

Second summer also means the added luxury of more whale sightings.

There are exceptions, of course (like the one autumn the SOLVE Beach Cleanup had to cancel due to a freak wind storm), but you'll generally find these inviting conditions going until about the middle of October – often a bit beyond. Temps linger around 70 or more, skies are blue, and winds can be nearly nonexistent.

For decades, this was a big secret. But since about 2000 or so, the popularity of the region during this month or two has gradually increased, so that now it's not uncommon to have even weekdays be full of visitors. Those grand, inviting conditions of second summer that were once known to just a few diehards have resulted in a lot more people. Basically, the secret is out.

Some towns still see some lodging price drops after Labor Day but now it's not as much as before the early 2000s. In fact, larger towns like Seaside, Lincoln City or Newport don't drop much – if at all – until the end of September.

However, most weekdays boast less people amid some truly balmy weather.

Once you get to early October, then crowds and lodging prices really drop off. The second summer phenomenon is still keeping things quite warm through the middle of the month. It's about October 15 when things move towards the blustery and rainy again, although in the last fifteen years there have typically been at least a few days scattered throughout October's last two weeks that remain remarkably warm, even tropical.

Travel officials say many more two-for-the-price-of-one specials start to pop up after September 15. It's also a good time to book conferences and meetings as prices for that can be lower.

A good rule of thumb is that the more expensive the place, the more it will drop in price. Less expensive hotels or motels will drop less.

So is this Second Summer real, you're asking? The science behind it is interesting.

According to meteorologists, the valley starts to cool off in September, but meanwhile the ocean waters off the coast have heated up over summer. This lessens the temperature differences between the two areas, and this helps keep things calmer (as those differences also drive things like wind and fog during the summer). Warmer winds from the valley can make it here more easily. On top of all that, warmer air from California is allowed to come up more by that action, which warms up the Oregon coast even more.

All this lack of wind, fog and generally nicer conditions make for waves that aren't very big. That is what you need to spot whales. September and October are usually incredible for whale sightings because the wave height doesn't hide them. Calmer conditions also coax them closer to shore, where they may be checking you out as well.

In recent years, gray whale numbers have been rather high during this whole second summer thing.

Early Spring of February

There's a semi-regular occurrence each February of unusually warm weather, nicknamed the Mini Spring of February. Sure, it's winter and that's generally a time of dreary, drenching weather. But stats show there are often about 10 days of dry conditions scattered throughout February, and these can get quite warm.

It doesn't occur every year and they're not consecutive days, but some years you have a run of downright balmy days, even warmer than many parts of summer. You'll get nearly no winds and lots of sun, and that can really heat things up. Temps will soar to close 60 degrees, sometimes beyond. And with no winds, that increases how warm you feel because there is no wind chill factor.

This is especially true on the sands. The beaches will feel much warmer, as much as 15 to 20 degrees warmer, because the sand and the ocean reflect the sun back. The temps in town can be 45 or maybe 55 degrees, and it can feel near 70 right at the tideline.

It's spectacular to encounter this.

The science behind it states that this is not all that unusual, except that on the coast, the moderate climate element can heighten the glorious weather factor.

Many areas of the United States will experience this, including inland Oregon. By this time of year, Oregon has gone through the early sunsets and the dark and wetter days. February begins to get over that hump, and the days are getting longer. That added sunlight heats up the weather just enough.

When those clear, sunny days of late winter happen – and it's not all the time, that's for certain – things are colder in the valley because of the east winds bringing colder air. In the valley it's that winter crisp: temps hovering around 40 to even freezing. On the coast, however, you can get temps more around 50, even on those near-32-degree days in the valley.

Basically, cold air settles in the valley. But on the coast, weather is automatically more moderate because it's next to the ocean, which is about 50 degrees, keeping things from straying too far away from that temperature. Even if it's raining heavily, it's often warmer on the coast than in the valley during the whole of winter, actually.

In the summer, this same element of the moderate ocean keeps the temperature down.

Again, it's important to remember this doesn't happen every year. You have to keep an eye on the weather reports. It's simply something to look out for.

Secret Spring

There's more to spring on the Oregon coast than spring break. In fact, that period after the main spring breaks - from mid April through to the end of May - is a distinctly unpopulated season with a host of interesting natural wonders that make this an unusual time of year on these beaches. It's nicknamed the "secret season," "hidden spring" or "secret spring" – various incarnations of that - because no one ever seems to talk about it. There is a growing movement of coastal businesses that are making it a point to speak up, however.

It's filled with a lot of wild wonders. From crazed sea foam, more fascinating creatures, empty beaches to really low tides and even Orcas.

Wild Weather Mood Swings. March and April bring a crazed kind of weather, often abruptly switching back and forth between sun and squalls within the same day, sometimes within a half hour. You get an interesting mix of increasingly nice days, with occasional winter-like storms still possible – periodically within the same day. May starts to calm down considerably, and you lose the big storms, but weather switch-a-roo's still happen quite often.

You'll want to come prepared for abrupt shifts in weather, bringing along changes in clothing and jackets, in case the weather decides to turn on you. In Lincoln City, you'll still have to watch those high tides during stormier days from a distance because of the width of the beaches.

Crazed Sea Foam Action. Spring storms can offer some wild, strange sights, especially when paired with the larger blooms of phytoplankton that happen this time of year. These are the microscopic creatures that whales and other fish eat in huge abundance. One kind, called diatoms, are the type of phytoplankton mostly responsible for the sea foam you see in the waves. Their millions of tiny skeletons combine with the air to make bubbles in the breakers. Basically, they make the sea foam.

With more foam because of the spring blooms, you then get a better chance of seeing sea foam pulling all sorts of strange stunts during the season's storms, like moving across the highways or even flying upwards, creating the mind-boggling sight of what looks like snow going the wrong direction.

Lincoln City is a great stretch of beach to spot this: nice and flat in many spots and the blobs of foam look especially graceful and beautiful as they glide along wet sand.

Also see Oregon Coast Spring Surprise: Now is Most Photogenic Time of Year: https://beachconnection.net/news/sprpho042313_623.php

Major Minus Tides. Some of the year's lowest minus tides can happen in March, April and May, with May having a tendency to be the lowest. This allows for greater exploration of Lincoln City's tidepools and other sights not always visible.

In some spots nearby, the landscape changes drastically in many ways at low tides. Entire new vistas of rocky marine gardens show themselves, such as at down at the Devil's Punchbowl near Depoe Bay, around Newport or up at Neskowin.

Lodging Prices Surprises. In the spring, around spring break, lodging prices start rising again after winter lows, but there's still this intermediate time where some remain at winter rates or just slightly higher. Lodging prices may even sometimes drop back down until May.

Spring lodging specials begin popping up like daisies, and that's where you can rake in the savings. Even if general rack prices don't drop back down.

Midweek savings packages are usually still around, and some inns remain 20 to 40 percent off their summer rates. See the Lincoln City Lodging page at BeachConnection.net, which features regular updates on such specials.

The Beaches Less Traveled. On top of the beautiful natural phenomena that abound this time of year, crowds are sizably less. In many beach burghs, it's almost a ghost town, even more so on the north Oregon coast. Neskowin really empties out as does Gleneden Beach. You can enjoy the most incredible chunks of the coastline in total solitude during this "secret spring" of April and May. You're apt to find the roads and beaches completely to yourself at times, if not fairly often. This is true even on most really nice weather weekends, where things do get a bit busier – but not much so.

Orcas. Killer whales often show up in April, usually lingering through May. See the previous chapter about whales.

Unusual Sights – Rarities in General

You haven't lived until you've made at least one really weird and stunning discovery along the Oregon coast. These can happen anywhere along this shoreline: glowing sand, double-headed sunsets, the famed Green Flash at Sunset and gobs more. Some are extremely rare, some are just fairly rare.

Glowing Sand. It's often mislabeled as "phosphorescence," however glowing sand is actually the result of tiny, bioluminescent forms of phytoplankton – meaning they glow in the same way fireflies do. What you see is a faint display of bluish / green sparks beneath your feet if you're walking in the wet sand at night. If you're lucky, it can almost look like a glow stick erupting for a few seconds, or it can show itself as a small, exploding galaxy beneath your feet if you stomp on a pool of water that's been around awhile.

You need a very dark beach to see this, one with little to no light interference. Lucky for you, Lincoln City and the areas surrounding it like Neskowin or Gleneden Beach come with plenty of dark beaches. Especially those two areas just north and south: they are pitch black. Some beaches get pretty heavily lit by some oceanfront hotels, but it's not too hard to walk out of that light source into a darker area.

Find more at www.BeachConnection.net on the subject.

Green Flash at Sunset. It's somewhat rare to extremely rare and it is one of the more coveted experiences. It's called the Green Flash at Sunset. The absolute right conditions have to be present. What you'll see is a brief green blob directly above the sun, just before the last sliver dips below the horizon. "Flash" is a bit of a misnomer as it tends to linger for at least a couple of seconds, sometimes nearly ten seconds. Every once in awhile, it turns the entire sliver of sun a weird green.

Contrary to popular belief, it doesn't just happen on a day with no clouds, although that's generally one of only two conditions where it's possible (see Novaya Zemlya section that follows). On really clear days, it helps to be on a high cliff. Lincoln City has plenty of those. For even more information on this and more full color photos, see www.beachconnection.net, then do a search on "green flash."

Novaya Zemlya Effect. Ever see a two-headed sunset? Or more than two? It's an unusual ocean weather phenomenon called the Novaya Zemlya effect, and it's considered quite a rarity around the rest of the world. But it may actually be more common on the Oregon coast, making this a rather special place.

This effect creates an illusion where it seems the sun is setting later than it really is. The upper part is often distorted in appearance, most of the time showing as a series of lighted bands across the sky. Yet you always see at least part of the real orb just below, descending down towards the horizon.

In the simplest terms, it's a kind of polar image mirage of the sunset.

Interestingly, since it works on many of the same scientific principles as the green flash, it can cause a green flash at sunset. Don't forget to look closely if you see this happening at the end of a pristine, calming day: you may have just doubled your chances of seeing the coveted green lighting effect. For even more information on this and more full color photos, see www.beachconnection.net.

Singing Sands. This actually happens mostly on two spots on the coast: in some areas of the National Dunes Recreation Area south of Florence and maybe - just maybe - south of Cannon Beach. Sometimes, it sounds like distant voices singing. Others, it's a bit like a violin. Then there's that elongated squishy, squeaking noise. All of it only happens under certain conditions, when two different kinds of sands grind together under the right degree of humidity.

Sorry, but all this generally happens about 100 miles to the north.

However, more frequent is the squeaking noise, and that is not necessarily limited to Cannon Beach. I've personally heard it at Tillicum Beach near Yachats and at Manzanita before. It seems that squeak is more common to Cannon Beach and nearby Arcadia Beach, but it's certainly possible to encounter it south of there, such as at Lincoln City.

There's more on it at www.BeachConnection.net and the other two books in this Ultimate Oregon Coast Travel series on Cannon Beach and Seaside.

Meteor Showers. There are few things more amazing than being on one of Lincoln City's beaches at night and spotting a lot of meteors. Once again, you'll need clear nights, which can be challenging on the coast. When nights here are clear – they're astoundingly clear. The stars are bright and the ring of the rest of the galaxy is spellbinding. Even if there are no meteor showers (like the Lyrids or others that regularly happen throughout the year), stray meteors are easy to see. If you're on the beach on a clear night, make sure you spend some time looking up.

The best areas for viewing the stars is anywhere in Lincoln City, really. They'll seriously stand out, however, on extremely dark beaches like Neskowin or Gleneden Beach.

DETAILED BEACHES AND LANDMARKS GUIDE

Neskowin

As you're zipping down 101 from Pacific City, at MP 98 the picturesque and mesmerizing village of Neskowin pops up, containing a handful of condos, a golf course, perhaps two or three businesses and a bundle of charming homes.

There is, at first glimpse anyway, not much at Neskowin. It's the beach that's the real attraction here: a long expanse of seriously pristine sand. But because of Neskowin's relative isolation, tucked away along a twisty stretch of highway, it's a treasure trove that's usually not very crowded.

Or – conversely – because it is small, it can be very crowded during summer.

Neskowin is also home of the famed 1,000-year-old to 1,900-year-old ghost forest stumps.

From the parking lot – technically Neskowin Beach State Recreation Site - it's a short walk to the beach and its slightly unusual dark grains of sand, plus enough driftwood to make yourself a decent fire.

Proposal Rock is the intriguing blob-like structure sitting in front of you, boasting a small forest sitting on top. There's a sizable creek between you and it, however, and to get to the structure means crossing this cold body of water barefoot.

Atop the rock, there are some hidden trails meandering through the forest where the views are somewhat legendary. Attempting this almost-aerial walkway is not recommended, however.

Watch the tides here closely or you could get stranded, and be extremely careful of the trail's slippery entrance.

Near the entrance, look for a small, round brass plaque, an oddity embedded there possibly decades ago. It bears the name of a power company, which means it was likely a survey marker. No one seems to know for sure what it is, but research on a similar brass marker at Cannon Beach's Hug Point revealed that one was a survey marker of some kind from the same power company. See the Cannon Beach book in this series, "Ultimate Oregon Coast Travel," or use the search feature at www.beachconnection.net for the terms "Hug Point brass knob."

Proposal Rock got its name from a young man that proposed to his girlfriend there early in the 20th century.

History: Wild Storm Surges of Neskowin

Upon entering the main beach access, you'll see this lovely little stream winding down to the ocean. Called Kiwanda Creek, it becomes Neskowin Creek out on the beach itself.

This area can be full of dangerous extremes, however.

This normally placid creek sits well back from the usual tide line in this tiny village: in fact the bridge over it – near the beach access – is a good quarter mile away from the ocean. It's here where most of the hotels sit, safely tucked away from the ocean at even its most chaotic.

Or are they?

Indeed, this chunk of the beach has been the recipient of some wild wave action in the past – under very rare circumstances. In the early 2010's, Proposal Rock Inn owner John Forsythe discovered a somewhat historical photograph of this area getting slammed by a big storm surge.

Even to the casual viewer, major debris in the creek lurking this far up the beach hints at the frightening power of the waves.

Late in 2010, there was still a huge, monstrous chunk of driftwood sitting way back here. Many visitors wouldn't give it a second thought. But if you know about ocean action to any degree, you give it quite the double take. What on Earth could bring such a monstrosity this far up the creek – about a quarter mile?

Back in October 2010, Forsythe explained.

"That debris came in on two storms last year," Forsythe said. "It was brought part way up the creek in December and later pushed to the bridge by a similar storm."

The debris has since been removed.

"Storm surges that combine with high tides can really bring the ocean up," Forsythe said. "Back in 1999 we had to replace our carpet as the ocean pushed our deck door open during a big event."

Mysterious Northern Sands

Northern Neskowin could well be the magnificent treasure of the tiny town, possibly competing with Proposal Rock and the Ghost Forest stumps.

Head north on Breakers Avenue and you start encountering westbound streets along the beachfront with the names of other Oregon towns, like Salem, Monmouth or Corvallis. Keep going about a mile beyond the first major curve and you'll find a small number of hidden beach accesses cloistered tightly between some homes. Even before the big curve, there are some accesses that are unbelievably beautiful - and devoid of people.

The final access at Corvallis Avenue is stunning. This northern section of Neskowin is so very different from the more populated state park access with all its funky features. There's a kind of mystical calm to it that is legendary: many claim the place simply feels different. Perhaps it's just the large, darker grains of sand that plunge rather abruptly into the surf and the distinct lack of others, or maybe it is an ethereal, slightly spiritual vibe that some people say it is.

There are unusually large amounts of broken shells littered about as well. Combined with the coarser sands, this makes walking barefoot somewhat uncomfortable.

Solitude is much more easily found here. You're literally miles from any other major beach. The sound and action of the surf seem to penetrate your consciousness more deeply in this placid place.

Neskowin's Ghost Forest

This downright spectacular oddity is almost a rare sight along the Oregon coast, and you may not know just how spectacular it is unless you know what you're looking at.

You have to cross the often-swift creek to get to it: it lies just beyond Proposal Rock. These ancient stumps are almost the only such ghost forest stumps you can see year-round, except for two much older examples at Otter Rock and Newport's Beverly Beach.

Other ghost forests sometimes appear in winter south of Newport and within town, at Cape Lookout State Park, Arch Cape and Hug Point. These are seasonal, however.

Like most of these ancient features, the Neskowin ghost forest stumps look somewhat like old, ragged pilings left over from something manmade - but they are, in fact, stumps of a forest some 1000 to 2000 years old or so. As many as 100 are sometimes visible in various shapes and sizes. It's theorized that around that time, the landscape changed rather quickly - in geologic terms - over a period of decades or perhaps all of a sudden. Sand, sea or muck covered this forest entirely, killing the trees. This wound up preserving them by hiding them from the decaying effects of oxygen, rather then destroying and scattering them as natural erosion might've done.

There were for awhile two schools of thought on the Neskowin ghost forest stumps: one saying the origin was a slower process that took decades (like most of the north coast stumps are proven to be); or a really sudden, scary one that involved a massive earthquake, the ground dropping abruptly and quite possibly a tsunami on top of all that.

In recent years, various media outlets erroneously have promoted the more cataclysmic theory. It's difficult to tell where that came from, as unfortunately no outlet actually quotes a known geologist on this. However, the work of Oregon's Curt Peterson and Roger Hart in the early 2000s is considered the definitive word: it was what is called gradual encroachment and not a sudden quake. It's much less exciting than the ground dropping 20 feet or more, but it's the truth.

This process - just like a quake event could have - immersed the stand of trees and thus preserved them.

They're not like the ghost forest stumps at Newport's Moolack Beach, which are just massive root systems some 4,000 years old. Apparently early settlers cut those trees down for wood supplies.

The ghost forest stumps of Neskowin are an eerie reminder, not just for their appearance but that quakes like the "big one" are still coming.

Are Neskowin's Ghost Forests in Danger?

2008 was a banner year for wild discoveries because of really low sand levels. The Great Gale of 2007 in December tore up lots of the north Oregon coast. It and other heavy storms scoured out so much sand some remarkable finds were possible, like the two 150-year-old cannon found near Cannon Beach, and even a mail truck from the '20s uncovered near Waldport.

But that year and a couple of years on either side began to spell trouble for the ghost forests of Neskowin.

Back then I interviewed beach ranger David Woody, with Oregon State Parks and Recreation Department – who is now retired. At the time he said the stumps at Neskowin were showing so much they were starting to get uprooted.

"I found some a ways up the road, at the beach at Winema," Woody said back then.

At the Oregon Department of Gem and Mineral Industries, geomorphologist Jonathan Allan and geologist Roger Hart said they were aware of several of these stumps being removed by erosion.

At the time Hart told me: "In my opinion, this past winter's erosion of the buried forests has been more severe than ever before. Waves have torn up Sitka spruce trees that were rooted in place for one to two thousand years at Neskowin, south of Proposal Rock, and at Cape Lookout State Park, along with great chunks of forest soil. They've strewn them all over beaches between Cascade Head and Cape Meares."

Normally, the ghost forest tree limbs and stumps at Neskowin collect barnacles and other sea life clinging to them during times when the tide surrounds it, especially after periods when sand levels have piled back up.

However, these specimens at Neskowin were getting exposed so much they were showing bare bark without sea life. It's ironic, since the opportunity to see them is the result of sand levels sinking low enough to expose them in the first place. They didn't appear to be showing year-round until the '90s, maybe later.

It's the same dynamic as many rocks at tide pools, where they suddenly show patches without sea life because sand levels have shrunk to expose an area that was normally off limits to these creatures. They haven't had the time to take over those sections.

"I've seen a lot of stumps without barnacles on them, where the sand has gone away," Woody said.

Fast forward a bit to 2011 and beyond, and suddenly those dramatic winter drops eased up. Ghost forests still emerged during winters around the coastline, some years more obviously than others. The tearing up action at Neskowin stopped, and now there seems to be a cycle of less erosion during winters, and longer calm periods that bring in more sand. Since about 2012 summers have been at higher and higher sand levels, making for broader, bigger beaches everywhere and unusual access to normally inhospitable attractions like the inside of the Devil's Punchbowl or a way around Oceanside's Maxwell Point without taking the tunnel.

The ghost forest at Neskowin has even been covered up for a time during some summers. For now, it doesn't seem in danger of getting scoured out. That could change, however, considering the unpredictable nature of a shifting climate, which is expected to include higher winter storm surges. Many coastal towns – including Lincoln City and Rockaway Beach – have been seeing larger storm surge events (see the storm history chapter later) and more damage to buildings and property.

In the late 2000's there was a cycle of heavier surf action, while the first half of the decade seemed a bit calmer. That could turn around again and it's possible that Neskowin's ghost forest could disappear some day.

History of the Village

The word "Neskowin" is tribal language for "plenty fish," because of the area's abundance of the slithery ones. It comes from the Nestucca band of Tillamook Indians that lived here. One historical anecdote talks about a creek here so full of fish one summer in the early 20th century that the waters were black.

The initial name given to the place by settlers was Slab Creek, with the first homestead created there about 1876. This was only after a few short years of the area being used as an Indian reservation. These original native residents weren't treated nicely when they were booted from the spot. In order to allow homesteaders, the U.S. government herded the indigenous people somewhere else again, moving them to the mouth of the Salmon River.

When the first settlers arrived in the late 1880s, they stole some of the wood from Nestucca burial canoes for use in building their homes. To add insult to injury, the bones contained therein were simply scattered on the ground.

Fishing was the village's only industry for years, then lumber for a time. Meanwhile, it never grew beyond a smattering of homes. One hotel - Neskowin Hotel - was built around 1895, but was nearly washed away. It was later moved a little more inland by blasting a spot out of the hillside. Proposal Rock Inn stands in its place now. Other hotels showed up in the late 1940s.

Proposal Rock was named after Charles Gage proposed to Della Page on it around the turn of the century. Della's mother, Sarah Page, so named the rock.

The first golf course was built in 1930, a year after electricity came to Neskowin. The road that later became Highway 101 was built in 1910. Somehow - primarily through the insistence of residents - Neskowin has hardly changed over the years, although now homes are slowly popping up all over. Still, no major development in terms of hotels and tourist traps are happening, and it remains this dusty gem in touristy terms.

Cascade Head and Trails

Take Three Rocks Road to one of the major trailheads for Cascade Head, or find some along that "corridor of mystery" where the road winds and turns beneath thick forestland.

This stately bluff was scooped up by the Nature Conservancy in the 1960s and has since been safe from commercial development. The result has been a pristine labyrinth of amazing trails and breathtaking viewpoints that will be with us for generations. However, dogs, camping, picking flowers and walking beyond designated boundaries (look for the signage that says so) is forbidden because of the delicate environmental balance here.

The most used trail is the Conservancy's 2.7-mile path, which takes you to some seriously gorgeous bluffs. That one's a 3.4-mile roundtrip from the lower trailhead, which you'll find along Savage Road, off Three Rocks Road.

The upper trailhead is much easier, although it's not open all year. It's shut down from January through May. But this one's only a two-mile roundtrip, accessible from Cascade Head Road, near MP 101, in Tillamook County.

The Hart's Cove Trail, also closed from January to May, is accessible by Cascade Head Road. Take the fork in the road to the north, then drive to its end, some four miles down. From that trailhead, the path meanders almost three miles through incredible views – including a waterfall - until you reach a bluff over a very secretive cove. You can reach it by heading down a steep and unpredictable path.

Startling Geology: Cascade Head is an Extinct Volcano

That resplendent visage of Cascade Head that graces the northern end of Lincoln City is a landmark with a truly fiery past. This now pleasant hiking experience was a big, mean and nasty monster once upon a time, something you would not have wanted to have been around. And yet somehow this is not talked about much.

But talk to Alan Niem, a retired OSU geology professor who now lives on the central Oregon coast, and you get a gush of knowledge about the headland.

The big plot twist: Cascade Head is an extinct volcano.

"Cascade Head was a submarine volcano, formed approximately 36 to 38 million years ago, based upon what we call radiometric dating of the lava rocks," Niem said.

It made for underwater eruptions during its existence, Niem said. Back then, the coastline was actually about 30 to 40 miles east of where it is now, which meant all this was in Spongebob Squarepants territory.

If you look at the underwater volcanoes off the Oregon coast right now, you'll get a glimpse into the past.

"They represent eruptions that probably happened like what we have today with the submarine volcanoes at Axial Ridge at Juan de Fuca spreading zone about 200, 300 miles offshore," he said.

However, this wasn't a spreading zone back then – meaning that currently the Axial Ridge offshore is where the two continental plates meet and grind against each other, and thus they cause volcanic activity. That kind of spreading wasn't happening in the area that Cascade Head was stewing and brewing. Back then, something else powered the volcano. More on that shortly.

Niem said scientists believe Cascade Head was something like 1,000 to 2,000 feet high at the time, and yet it was still 1,000 feet beneath the ocean surface. It stopped erupting around 36 million years ago.

In a few ways, it's not unlike what's happening in Hawaii now. It was what they call a seamount – an underwater volcano.

Having been underwater, eruptions like this create a lot of pillow basalt, which is the rounded, bubble-like basalt rocks you see at Depoe Bay that happen because lavas meet with water. The eruptions happened pretty deep and far off the continental shelf and slope at that time, creating not just pillow basalts but breccias too (pronounced bre-chias), which are fragmented rocks often mixed with other rocks.

"But it wasn't very explosive, nothing like Mount St. Helens; probably more of a quiet eruption, more like what you get in Hawaii," Niem said. "But Hawaii is a big, huge volcano that built up above the waterline. In this case, we have no evidence that this volcano reached above sea level."

In fact, part of how they know this is that the top of the old volcano is covered in a younger rocky material called the Nestucca Formation, which contains micro fossils. Those fossils and other dating of that mudstone sediment material show it was all part of the ocean floor much later on.

There were also lava dikes all over the area – which is where hot magma and molten rock erupted from different spots around the volcano and squeezed up through cracks in the surface.

In fact, there is one significant lava dike visible at Lincoln City's Nelscott district, and it's about a half mile or more north of the SW 33rd Ave. access. It holds a lot of agate veins that are responsible for many of the agate finds in this central Oregon coast town.

It's not for certain, but evidence points to the Cascade Head eruptions as causing this blob of basalt in town. It's another – probable – remnant you can see of all this wild volcanic action.

Niem said that around the middle late Miocene – about 13 to 11 million years ago – the whole former volcano and the sediment on top was uplifted above the water. After that, all kinds of erosion took place: by weathering, by rivers cutting through the softer sedimentary rock, and also landslides. You can see evidence of that when you hike up to the top of Cascade Head: in some places about 500 feet of landslides are evident. The famed God's Thumb is clearly one big landslide. The softer parts were removed first and then millions of years took care of the rest of the old volcano cone.

"So it left this volcanic high," he said. "It's no longer a volcano shape, just an erosional remnant."

The volcano action itself took place in what's called the Eocene – an epoch about 36 million to 45 million years ago.

This was a time after another enormous set of eruptions farther up what would become the Oregon coast: a series of underwater eruptions that created the Tillamook Highlands. These appear to have been about several thousand feet high and actually did rise above the water and formed big islands, like what Hawaii is now. These stretch from Pacific City all the way up to nearly Rockaway Beach, and as far east as the coast range. Those happened about 40 to 43 million years ago.

Those eruptions and the later Cascade Head all seem to have been powered by the same hotspot in the Earth that now fires up Yellowstone National Park. At around 18 million years ago, that spot also created the Columbia Basalts, which were massive lava flows that moved all across Oregon from 300 miles away and made it into the waters of what we now know as the Oregon coast. The Columbia Basalts lavas were what created most of the well-known landmarks such as Neahkahnie Mountain, Cape Meares, Tillamook Head and so on.

During all this, the continental plates were moving, but not just westward. Around the time of the Tillamook Highlands and Cascade Head eruptions, the plates were moving in a southwest direction, or clockwise. That weak spot in the crust always stayed in the same spot, however. That's why the big eruptions moved around: the continent drifted over it.

How did geologists come these conclusions? Niem said they know this through geochemical evidence, isotopes and looking at the kinds of rocks that are strewn around and where they are. All that has provided plenty of evidence to researchers.

It's interesting to note, Niem said that around 20 to 40 million years ago, Oregon was a tropical place.

"All the indications are that Oregon had a tropical climate like that of Hawaii, or Acapulco, Mexico, based on flora and plants found in coal beds found in places like Washington," Niem said.

What's the future of Cascade Head? It's slowly – very slowly – falling apart.

Once Cascade Head stopped erupting, it was soon covered by sediments from the bottom of the ocean, which later became what is called the Nestucca formation. It and the area south of it, around the northern tip of Lincoln City, are a mix of what is left of that formation and some basalt (there are some giant basalt caves between Lincoln City and Three Rox Bay that you can't see).

Back in 1974, Oregon geologist Ernest Lund wrote the Nestucca formation is eroding quickly. Some day, those basalt chunks will be separate from the land areas known as Cascade Head and Roads End. In fact, the Three Rocks of Three Rox Bay are what the area will look like eventually.

Odd History: the Shipwreck and Skeleton of Three Rox Bay

A host of mysteries lurk just north of Lincoln City, inside the little bay beneath Cascade Head.

It all started in the 1700s – or 1932 – depending how you think about it. It's a tale of murder, sex, local native legends, a skeleton of an eight-foot giant, possibly a pirate ship, a search for treasure and a local family caught up in the middle of it.

Thanks to bundles of information from the North Lincoln County Historical Museum, there's a pretty clear record of much of this intriguing mystery. According to articles archived by the museum, homesteaders who settled in the Lincoln City and Neskowin areas had long heard legends from local tribes about a shipwreck and a mysterious black man briefly worshiped as a god. These tales are documented all the way back to the mid 1800s, and just before the Calkins family started settling into the bay where the Salmon River dumps out to sea next to Cascade Head.

The son of that family, Elmer Calkins, began laying the groundwork for his own homestead near Cascade Head in 1932, according to a 1972 article in the LA Times. As he plowed the ground in preparation for building he ran across something quite unusual: human bones.

Elmer, according to the LA Times article, had grown up with local tribes people all around him and he knew their ways. So what made this find even more striking was that the bones were buried with discarded sea shells. This was, after all, the Indians' form of a garbage dump. They did not bury their dead in garbage piles.

Stranger still, one of the three skeletons was a giant. The man – later discovered to be African – was eight feet tall.

Calkins quickly contacted historian Dr. John Horner and the local coroner, Dr. F. M. Carter. Historical photos from the North Lincoln County Historical Museum show them examining the burial site. Horner took them back to Oregon State University in Corvallis and dated the skeletons at about 160 years, which would have placed them on the central Oregon coast around the late 1700s.

The other two skeletons were of Caucasian men.

Meanwhile, something immediately clicked with local historians and with Calkins. They had heard many of the tales handed down from generations. One of them was of a gigantic "winged canoe" that came into the bay next to Cascade Head. The timeline of that legend matched up with the 160-year-old bones.

The legend said the crew of the ship wandered off inland after the wreck and were never heard from again. Three stayed behind: two white men and the giant African man.

In the LA Times article, Calkins vividly remembers the tale.

"The Indians worshiped the black giant, so the legend went," Calkins said at the time. "They were in awe of the man because of his color and his size."

Then, the natives decided that perhaps this man was not a god, and they turned against him. Children were suddenly being born to the women of the tribe with distinctly African features.

"When the Indians decided the giant was human they killed him and his two shipmates," Calkins said of the legend.

In a show of contempt, the bodies were thrown into the kitchen middens – the piles of shells from seafood the tribes lived on.

Calkins also noted many of the local tribal people he grew up with around the turn of the century had some African features, such as dark, curly hair.

Interestingly enough, this wasn't Calkins' first encounter with real life evidence of the legend. Years before, while gillnetting in that bay (Calkins is actually also responsible for getting the bay the name of Three Rox Bay), his net snagged on part of the rib of a sunken ship.

That discovery created a small media sensation in the 1920s, and Calkins told the LA Times people flooded the area trying to dig up what they thought would be a pirate's booty.

In 1974 – two years after the LA Times piece – Salem's The Capital Journal (the precursor to the Statesman Journal) ran a story about Calkin's son, Ed Calkins. The younger Calkins was about to embark on something that sounded like a sub plot in the series "The Curse of Oak Island." He too had caught treasure fever and in 1974 applied for a dig permit from the state of Oregon.

In that article, the younger Calkins said he believed the ship to be a pirate ship that tried to hide in this area, running from the British. It also notes how Calkins had apparently detected gold and silver with a metal detector around that wreckage.

The article said one of the skulls of the human remains was still pierced with an arrowhead, while another man apparently had had his head crushed with a rock.

There are striking similarities between this giant skeleton and its history and the legends of a shipwreck on the north Oregon coast at Manzanita. It's been proven a Spanish ship wrecked near Manzanita in the 1700s and local native legends about it are quite varied. Some of those legends, however, talk about a tall black man as being part of the crew, and one version even says he was buried alive with a supposed "treasure" to ward off interference from Indians.

It begs the question that perhaps this Manzanita story was an offshoot of the more verifiable facts of the Lincoln City discoveries.

More on the Lincoln City shipwreck and giant skeleton history is available when visiting the North Lincoln County Historical Museum. 541-996-6614.

Corridor of Mystery

That stretch between Neskowin and the Highway 18 junction that whizzes past Cascade Head has been sometimes referred to as the "Corridor of Mystery" by some locals and regular visitors, because of its thick canopy of trees and a sense of the impenetrable all around you. It's lush and gorgeous, but it's also a white-knuckled drive full of hills, twists and turns where you really have to pay attention. So it seems like you're missing out on the scenery around you, and the little nooks and crannies of forest features that zoom quickly past.

Probably hence the mystery.

This section also includes markers for the 45th Parallel, which is the point halfway between the equator and the north pole.

Highway 18

It technically all begins at Highway 18, some 70 miles away. Along Highway 18, outside Portland, you'll encounter the lush Yamhill wine country and quaint towns like Dundee. There's also charming McMinnville, with Howard Hughes' Spruce Goose in a museum, an interesting arts community, some fine culinary pleasures and a quaint old downtown area.

Along the way, it's wine-tasting heaven, with some of the nation's finest wine makers populating this grand and awe-inspiring region. This is a gargantuan distraction all its own and could take days to explore if you wanted to really dig in, but you'd still only glimpse about half of what Oregon's achingly beautiful and scrumptious wine country has to offer.

At Grande Ronde, near the casino, Highway 22 from Salem meets up with Highway 18 and heads through the lush forestland of the Van Duzer Corridor until it wanders past Otis and enters Lincoln City.

Coming from the North

Neskowin is the next little town, about 20 miles north of Lincoln City. There's also the colossal Cascade Head, with its mind-bending array of hiking possibilities. Just north of all that, sits Pacific City and Cape Kiwanda. The coastline stretches over 100 miles until it dead-ends at the Columbia River and Astoria, hosting towns and features like the Three Capes Tour, Tillamook Bay, Bay City, Garibaldi, Rockaway Beach, the mystical Nehalem Bay, Wheeler, Manzanita, Arch Cape, Cannon Beach, Seaside and Gearhart. See www.beachconnection.net for even more, and the other books in this series.

Otis

You'll encounter this tiny town just a few miles before reaching Lincoln City. It's famous for the legendary breakfasts of the Otis Café.

History: Pixieland and Pixie Kitchen

On Highway 101, not far from the Highway 18 junction, you'll find a plaque showing where Pixieland was. If you blink, you'll miss it. The whole tale actually begins with Pixie Kitchen (see that chapter later).

Pixieland seems to have grown in mythology and glowing fondness over the decades, almost rivaling how big it was in real life. The 53-acre park wasn't around long and never really attracted that many visitors, and the trips down memory lane seem to forget that. People talk much these days how they miss it, but they're likely among those who didn't attend as much as they think they did.

But that's OK. It's a unique phenomenon and it shouldn't be forgotten.

At its heyday – which was awfully brief - it boasted a dozen or so rides, a sizable park for trailer campers next door, and a smattering of eatery booths. Rides like the Grunykinland put you in the arms of a giant bear and sent you into a dark area lit by black lights that was supposedly the home of the pixies. There was a log flume that got you slightly wet, some bumper cars, and a train that meandered around the property.

Pixieland opened its doors to much fanfare in 1969, with an appearance by Governor Tom McCall. It was on land that

Pixie Kitchen owner Jerry Parks had purchased in 1966, set on a sprawling wet lands area near the junction of Highway 101 and Highway 18. Nothing of it is visible now: nature has reclaimed the whole thing.

Parks acquired it as a backup plan because he was certain a bypass would be built around the main drag of Highway 101 in Lincoln City, thus cutting off his Pixie Kitchen from the tourist throngs. But that never happened.

So up this vision of pixies on the coast went: but cracks in it showed pretty quickly.

There are plenty of interesting anecdotes about it. Among them, that Paul Newman visited there in 1971 during the filming of Sometimes a Great Notion.

Ed Dreistadt, director of Lincoln City's visitors center, has become a bit of an expert on the place.

He recalls Parks' daughter, Sharon Walters, telling the story of when they were in the middle of some construction in its early days, with the help of her husband, Howard. One day, a dump truck was dropping dirt near the train trestle that the park's little choo choo ran on.

"The driver forgot to put the bed down, and started driving out of the park and took out the trestle," Dreistadt said. "Sharon was working at the park's restaurant at the time and heard a horrible noise. So she had to call down to where Howard was at another end of the park and told them to not let the train leave."

There was a lot of enthusiasm and optimism for Pixieland for even the first two, three years: even by the second year, when problems began to be evident, everyone plowed right ahead. They simply began work on fixing the various issues. One thing, however, seriously eluded them: turning a profit. The right "formula" for grabbing enough visitors to really turn things around was somehow never within reach.

By 1971, serious cracks began to show, including Parks lowering his own salary. They slowly began trying a flurry of new things, including selling longterm lots at the trailer park and a variety of changing rides. In 1972, the Salmon River flooded parts of the complex. A Ferris wheel came and went, they began charging admission, and suddenly in 1973 Parks openly complained the operating season was too short and that the amusement park was too far from a major population center like Portland.

Dreistadt remembers a man who gave him a DVD of some home movies made there, somewhere around 1974.

"There was no one there," Dreistadt said. "It's like he had this whole amusement park to himself."

In 1975, the end was quickly en route. In some ways, this is when the place shut down. Although it seems it didn't technically shutter its glittery gates until 1977. Parks announced a two-year phase-out in '75. By that time, Pixieland was in visible decay; it was obvious the abandoned buildings were becoming an eyesore.

In '76, the U.S. Forest Service was looking to restore all the wetlands in the area, including the land Pixieland sat on. When the government got wind that part of their new business plan included more construction and a new development, they began to pounce, eventually by condemning the property which in turn allowed the agency to buy the land for pennies on the dollar later on.

A series of backroom deals and shuffling of papers and finances went on behind the scenes for a bit, but in 1978 the corporation was considered dead.

In the end, it seems a multitude of factors went into the fairy tale's demise: high cost of upkeep in the salt air, maybe some mismanagement, but mostly the inability to attract enough patrons to turn a healthy dime.

These days, some bits of the mythical attraction are scattered about in the oddest places. Two of the whale boat cars can be seen in front of the Anchor Inn in Lincoln City. A train still putts around in Utah these days. There's a whole Facebook group dedicated to the place which occasionally shows memorabilia belonging to someone.

Curiously, long after Pixie Kitchen was gone more fairy tidbits emerged. The building became a bar named Hershey's that burned down in the '90s, and numerous items from the park and the restaurant were discovered – most of which mysteriously grew legs and disappeared.

History: How Lincoln City Was Formed

Like superheroes, even towns have their origin stories.

This long, slender town that hugs the coastline has quite the history of how it was formed – and quite the fight over what eventually became its name. Currently, the town is about seven miles long and about a mile and a half wide, from shoreline to eastern boundary. It's a tourism hotspot that's essentially been that way for decades, although it had a somewhat disjointed start.

North Lincoln County Historical Museum in Lincoln City managed to rustle up a bundle of documents on the subject, and it's a fascinating trip through time. It's really best told in two parts that are tightly intertwined: how it was formed and how it was named (in the next chapter).

What most people don't know is that the town is of a fairly recent origin: it came about in 1964. This is unlike most other

Oregon coast burghs, which came into being around 100 years ago. It's also comprised of a bunch of little communities that merged together as one – under some duress.

The very first communities in this area sprouted up from between 1896 to 1935, which included the villages of Kernville (to the immediate southeast), Cutler City, Taft, Oceanlake and Nelscott, along with the short-lived Wecoma Beach. They were considered officially founded when their local post offices came into being. They weren't officially incorporated, however. Incorporation happened with Oceanlake in 1945, and then Taft and Delake in 1949.

Wecoma Beach never got that chance. A series of annexation attempts by Oceanlake finally made Wecoma part of that little town in 1955, but not before three different elections, one court case where the absorption was actually thrown out, and a long, bitter struggle by both sides.

By that time, the animosity generated by the annexation along with some sketchy bookkeeping practices in the area caused locals to begin to consider consolidating all five little burghs: Cutler, Taft, Oceanlake, Delake and Nelscott.

Historians sometimes talk about seven little communities banding together, probably referring to Neotsu and the already-absorbed Wecoma. Roads End was also another unofficial community, so in a way it was actually eight merging. However, it was those aforementioned five that actually voted on the proposals.

The idea was that auditing of city government money could be better done under one flag, so to speak, and there were the issues of obtaining a more efficient local government, better streets and mail service. Improved police and fire protection, along with hospitals, were also on the minds of locals.

Interestingly enough, while most historians note the main elections on consolidation and even the name of the five conjoined towns happened in 1964, according to Oregon Coast History Center's Steve Wyatt (in Newport), there was actually an election held about 1949 or so.

The idea was first brought up in 1948 at a Legion Hall in Taft, according to Wyatt's research. Even then, the small think-tank on the issue decided Lincoln City would be the best name for the new town. But editor of the North Lincoln County News, Jerry Stitter, immediately railed against the moniker. He published an editorial on December 6, 1948, that was highly critical: a foreshadowing of what was to come.

The very first vote on the subject came around '49. Wyatt, in a 2000 article written for a Newport publication, said the vote came four months after that legion hall meeting. With everyone in those communities voting, they "turned down the proposed consolidation by 374 votes, a margin of 2.5 to 1," Wyatt wrote.

This concept came up again and was once more not well received by some, and it too began another drawn-out battle. Yet the margins narrowed considerably. The first vote in May of 1964 failed because of only seven no votes by residents of Taft.

On December 8 of 1964 the votes finally came through: all five would become a single town. This time, Taft carried the measure by three votes.

Soon after the election, a charter form of government was created with councilmen from each of the five burghs, plus a sixth councilman-at-large - and they even elected a mayor. This all took place on March 5, 1965, with Ross Meyer becoming the first mayor. He served until 1971, according to a 1998 article by Gail Kimberling of The News Guard. She interviewed Meyer's successor, J.B. "Bud" Kiefer, at the end of the century.

Kiefer is quoted as saying: "I was dumb enough to accept, but smart enough to know what to do with the position."

Through his time in office, the little Oregon coast town made a ton of civic improvements, fighting what he called the "no growth policies" at the time. Kiefer had to deal with much in the beginning, such as a warning from the state Attorney General that Lincoln City had not had a financial audit in five years, and the discovery he couldn't make phone calls out of his city hall office because there weren't enough phone lines.

He served until 1978.

Odd History: How Lincoln City Was Named

A Lincoln City is a Lincoln City by any other name, right?

Well, maybe. Probably. The central Oregon coast hotspot had quite the bumpy, winding and twisting beginnings a little over half a century ago – see the previous chapter.

Deciding upon the name of Lincoln City is its own awkward, meandering historical tale. It all began with talk of consolidating five little beach burghs into one bigger one, as far back as 1948. In 1964, the town was finally formed from the joining of tiny neighboring communities that went by the names of Taft, Oceanlake, Delake, Nelscott and Cutler City.

In fact, those names still adorn their former villages but are now referred to as neighborhoods or sections of town that go by those monikers. Other areas once separate but which were never incorporated into towns still go by the neighborhood names of Wecoma, Neotsu or Roads End.

The first discussions of melding them all into one happened late 1948. Even then, the favored moniker was Lincoln City, and there's a some evidence in the documentation that city founders would stick to that no matter what, in spite of public input later on.

Not all were in favor of that name, however. Editor of the North Lincoln County News, Jerry Stitter, immediately railed against the name. He published an editorial on December 6, 1948 that was pretty snarky on the subject.

Back then, Stittser said that suggestion was "too hackneyed," meaning far too common. He noted there were already so many places in America with Lincoln in their names. He suggested Grand View, since that had been a potential name for the area around Schooner Creek back when settlers first arrived in the 1880s. He reaffirmed this argument by pointing out residents had a "grand view of the sea and of the lofty timber-mantled hills or of the placid waters of Devil's Lake" (according to an article in 2000).

The first vote by the small communities happened in 1949, the second two happened 15 years later in '64.

At that time, residents were far from convinced of the handle of Lincoln City as the electoral decision started kicking into gear. According to a News Guard article in 1999, quoting then-North Lincoln Historical County Historical Museum curator Katrina Pool, she (among other sources) say there were contests held for the public to decide the new name for the proposed town. The News Guard and radio station KBCH ran the contest in March of 1964, which brought in over 300 potential names. A committee then narrowed them down to five choices: Miracle Beach, Miracle City, Surfland, Holiday Beach and Lincoln City. (There actually already is a Holiday Beach just south of Newport).

Like Stittser, much of the public objected to it too, based on the same reasons of lack of originality.

The committee had the final say, and it struggled between "Lincoln City," which had won the public contest by two to one - and Surfland, which the majority of the school kids in the area were fond of. Somehow, the comment that Surfland was too "honky tonk" made by someone tipped the scales and it was dropped in favor of Lincoln City.

Yes, the town was nearly called Surfland, Oregon.

As the final vote at the end of '64 sealed the consolidation deal, by that time the controversial handle of this Oregon coast town was solidified.

Still, as one historian put it: "it was a non-controversial solution to the often thorny surviving name problem." No one was happy about the entire city adopting the name of the one of the smaller towns that comprised it.

The name problem did not go away. For decades. In March of 1967, the News Guard wrote about another movement by disgruntled residents to change the name of the Oregon coast burgh. This time, polls taken by the newspaper found 116 wanted to keep the name while another 102 wanted to change it to Lincoln Shores.

Obviously defeated down the line, the article has a special cutout poll – like the coupons of old - to send in to city managers stating whether you were or were not in favor of an election on a name change.

The idea popped up again in 1999 as Newport's Steve Wyatt – head of the Oregon Coast History Center - wrote an article about past renaming issues. In 1999, the favored name was "Beach City." The idea was revisited once more in 2015, but again nothing came of it.

It makes you ponder what might've been. If the multiverse theories of physics are correct, somewhere there are universes out there where there's a Surfland on the Oregon coast, a Beach City and maybe even a Grand View, Oregon.

You can see more about the history of Lincoln City at the North Lincoln County Museum.

History: Site of Pixie Kitchen, Wecoma Beach (Lincoln City), Oregon

Between NW 36th St. and NW 35th St., next to the big credit union building, is where the famed Pixie Kitchen was. Now, it's a coffee stand surrounded by a parking lot and pavement.

The whole saga of the Pixie Kitchen and Pixieland started in the late '40s. Jerry Parks and a biz partner owned the Crab Broiler Restaurant in Seaside then, which burned down around 1950. They rebuilt the place, only to sell it shortly after. The family moved around a bit, including California, only to return to Oregon in 1952, and buying up a little restaurant in what was then called Wecoma Beach, Oregon.

That restaurant already had the name Pixie Kitchen, but the food specialized more in chicken pot pies. When Parks and his wife Lu got hold of it, they set about changing the name, but an instant public uproar from locals over what they already considered a landmark shut that idea down immediately. Pixie Kitchen remained just that.

There was an upstairs apartment the family intended to use, but it was in rather shoddy condition. So Parks and his wife sent the kids to live with their grandparents in Newberg for a time as they remodeled it.

In the meantime, the '50s meant a fair amount of expansion, and the restaurant slowly added on buildings basically cobbled together from other buildings next door.

Parks retained the rights to his menu at the old spot in Seaside and set about capitalizing on fried fish. According to many accounts this was the first – or certainly among the very first – restaurant to go to an all-you-can-eat format.

Reportedly, this format meant that when you ordered seconds, you were given a much bigger portion to "make sure" you'd had enough, Dreistadt said.

"It was mostly fried fish," Dreistadt said. "Fish was dirt cheap in this part of the country back then. Parks had deals where he'd buy entire catches from boat captains in Depoe Bay. But around the mid '60s, grocery stores like Safeway or Albertsons or whatever started carrying breaded and frozen fish – like fish sticks. All of a sudden these chains were buying up all the seafood and the price went through the roof. His business model fell apart. He couldn't make money like he did."

The '60s meant the expansion of the Pixies idea. Little animatronics were added here and there of Pixies and other characters. The front entrance had a wacky distorted mirror that made you look skinny, with the sign saying you were clearly hungry. On the way out was a mirror that made you look bigger and a sign that that essentially you said "you look full now."

At one point, around the late '60s, Pixie Kitchen was considered one of the top grossing restaurants in the entire nation, down to the top one percent. Throughout much of its existence, two-hour waits were not uncommon to get in to eat.

One of its missions was to keep kids entertained. A Pixie garden was created out back. It was a prerequisite for employment there to know how to run the little ones around and work off some of their energy.

About this time George Bruns came into the picture. He and Parks were friends since the '30s, and together the pair had been involved in booking jazz bands and were in other parts of the music biz. By the '60s, however, Bruns was a bigwig at Disneyland, composing major songs for the park's attractions like Pirates of the Caribbean and the song "Ballad of Davy Crockett" among others. He also composed or arranged many Disney films, like Sleeping Beauty and he created the theme for The Love Bug.

In fact, Bruns saved Disneyland in its early days. It looked iffy back then, but when he added Dixieland nights the park suddenly went into the black.

Bruns started creating songs for the animatronics at Pixie Kitchen, and went on to do the tunes for some of the rides at Pixieland. It's a connection to Parks and his two operations that still stuns people today.

Parks was ever the publicity and gimmick hound. He knew how to create a buzz. This included having a gibbon – a smallish ape – goofing around the restaurant.

"It was a weird ape with long arms," Dreistadt said. "Sharon and her mom used to take it on walks on the beach. It was an attraction they kept in the basement. As it got a little older, it got mean and started biting people, so they had to make it go away."

The story goes it went back to the zoo in Portland where it came from in the first place.

In the late '60s, Pixieland was created, and that – as illustrated in a previous chapter – was not exactly a rousing success. By 1977 it was gone.

Two years later, Jerry and Lu sold the restaurant and retired to Newberg, where Jerry grew up. At one point after 1980, the eatery was in financial dire straits and went to a buffet model and a much smaller staff.

In later interviews, their daughter Sharon said she knew fairly quickly the new restaurant wasn't going to succeed. It shut down in 1983, and a brief revival in 1985 by other owners did not pan out.

Jerry and Lu had both passed away by '93 and are inurned in Dundee, Oregon.

About 1990, the building became a wacky bar named Hershey's. That building burned down in the mid '90s. The reason is a bit juicy. As some accounts go, there was an employee who lived in the apartment upstairs with his girlfriend. One night, upon finding out she was being cheated on, she set fire to the bed in a fit of rage.

Interestingly enough, a bar in West Salem that existed briefly wound up with the booth seating from that Lincoln City bar. It was shut down not long after a riot in 2001. I can personally attest to this part. I'd had a few drinks at Hershey's in '92, and the red, kind of seedy booths stuck with me. Several years later, while working as the nightlife writer for Salem's Statesman Journal, I was chatting with the owner of this bar in West Salem and he bragged about getting a deal on the furniture. When he said where they from I immediately recognized them. Apparently, they were one of the few objects in the bar not ruined by smoke.

For further reading on the subject, it's recommended you see Mike Stone's book "Pixies in the Valley."

Devil's Lake State Recreation Area and Campground

Head south onto East Devil's Lake Rd. to reach this favorite camping, fishing and boating spot. There are 50 tent sites, 10 yurt spots, a great number of electrical and full hook-up sites that can even have cable TV, paved parking and a load of other amenities in the campground. There's also a hiker/ biker camp. This is the northern access to the lake.

The lake is so named by local natives because of a purported monster that inhabited it. Full information at oregonstateparks.org or (800) 551-6949.

Sparky the Wish Guardian

He stands about twice the height of a human – but he also stands high in the eyes of some national art critics.

The Devil's Lake Creature in Lincoln City – a massive metallic creature also known as "Sparky the Wish Guardian" – was put into place here back in 2013. The whimsical sculpture sits above Devils Lake at Regatta Grounds Park, residing at the entrance. He looks a bit like a happy-go-lucky cylon from Battlestar Galactica, or a chubbier, more cherubic relative of Robby the Robot.

Sparky towers over his human creators at 13 feet high and 18 feet long, visible at quite a distance away. The creature itself is comprised of 90 percent recycled material including steel, car metal, round bar, and retread tires. Local artists Heidi Erikson and Doug Kroger created the little big guy, after the Lincoln City Public Arts Committee sought them out and commissioned them.

The Devil's Lake Creature was a unique project for the pair of artists. Transporting him took lots of caution and care to prevent any damage. Each piece was galvanized separately. During its dedication back in 2013, you could "put a wish" into the heart of the creature.

Being located along the Oregon coast, it is subject to the seasonably wet weather of the Pacific Northwest and to the harsh salt sea air as well as the moist air from the lake.

A few months after installation, it was selected by the American Galvanizers Association (AGA) as a winner of the 2013 Excellence in Hot-Dip Galvanizing Awards. Sparky crowded out more than 120 impressive projects that were submitted, representing a variety of applications of hot-dip galvanizing with all of the projects being judged online by a panel of architects and engineers.

Roads End State Recreational State

At this the very northern tip of Lincoln City, it's appropriately called the Roads End district and Roads End State Recreational Site. This is where the town simply stops, butting up against a headland called Roads End Point that seems to slightly echo the shape of Cascade Head just beyond it and the prominent God's Thumb formation in the distance. This is the last public beach access before you have to drive 15 or so miles north to hit the Three Rocks Road area.

Well, there's one more secret beach access just north of here. More on that in a bit.

Roads End State Rec Site is a sizable parking lot elevated above this comely sandy stretch, coming complete with restrooms and some grassy areas that allow for your fur babies to do their business. Make sure you clean up after them, of course.

That grassy area at the eastern edge was actually once the spot of a famed restaurant for decades, one with a decidedly killer view. But it burned down in the early 2000's. This wound up beneficial to the general public as it opened up the view, and now there's even more parking spots available for beachgoers.

Many of the town's real surprises lie at Roads End. From here, you can keep taking Logan Road northward through a neighborhood of stunning cabins and extravagant homes until it all ends in a gated area. There are two more tiny public accesses hiding between the homes, which helps if you want to walk all the way to the end of the state park to its cave and piercing Wizard Rock, as that's a bit of a hike from the main access. Actually, it's almost a mile and a half, so for the usually casual walker anything but the final two tiny accesses will be a leg-cramper, and thus these can be a necessity.

Along the way, note the wild scratchings in the cliffs: signs of one kind of geologic struggle or another. Then there are the really trippy surprises of a kind of mini-bay hiding in plain sight and something else unusual the sea water has been known to do here. More on those next.

At the very end of this walk, you finally bump into tidepools and a dense gathering of basalt rocky globs and blobs. There's also Wizard Rock. But apparently it's not the slightly blunted and bumpy spire close to you – the one that's directly in front of you and which has often been mislabeled as Wizard Rock. There's a truly poky spire beyond here that's just out of sight – and that's the real Wizard Rock.

Standing in this spot, you'll see there's something just over the rocky slabs at the tip of the point. Indeed, there's even a cool, mysterious cave. This area hides the actual Wizard Rock and that cave, and it is largely inaccessible.

Under very rare circumstances can you get around this, when high sand levels coincide with extremely low tides, but by and large it's a place almost never seen by humans. Your drone might make it, however. There is one chunk of rock that people often use to try and get to it, but it's technically not allowed. If park officials see you they'll stop you. It's only doable if you don't fear the ultra-tiny strip of rock that everything narrows into – so tiny it's not even something that can be crawled. Falling and cracking your head here is far too easy to do.

Very simply: it's just too dangerous. Don't try it. And even if you do make it, you not only have to make it back without wrecking yourself but you have to worry about tides trapping you in that cave or the cove.

Still, the big attraction of this section of beach is that it's so remote you'll rarely find others. The angular rock formations here are fun to climb on for a ways, the tidepools are engaging, and if agates are to be found you can be sure nary another soul has picked them clean.

Secret Accesses: 66th St. and 7200 Block

Just beyond the main park, up Logan Road, two more secret accesses grant you passage to the sands. They're tiny and they're extremely difficult to find. One, without any parking, is simply a path between homes around 66th St.

The other is marked as a day use spot around the 7200 block of Logan Road, and it features maybe two parking spots on the concrete. Both are about a quarter mile north of the main parking lot, so you're cutting a little out of your strenuous hike to the end of the beach and its secrets – but not much.

The big caveat here: be cautious and courteous as you park as it is after all someone else's neighborhood. Don't block driveways and don't litter. Don't be a jerk in general.

At the 66th St. access, you'll have to park on the side of the road, preferably on 66th itself (since everything else is more or less parking in front of people's homes). At the northern access, you'll likely have to do the same.

Odd Fact: Lincoln City Hides a Second Bay

There is what could be termed yet a second bay in this central Oregon coast resort town: almost another little cozy cove, aside from the more well-known and even famous Siletz Bay at the southern side. Very loosely speaking, it's a kind of a cove, and not something even officially recognized by the city or visitors bureau. But it is a fun and funky little geographic delight you've likely never noticed before, and yet it's very real.

At the very northern tip of Lincoln City you'll find the appropriately named Roads End area, another district of town that is practically tucked away and where the town dead-ends up against a headland neighboring the more famous Cascade Head. Secure yourself a spot in the parking lot at this state park and walk a ways northward – and if you're lucky you may find it.

The sand here moves in curious ways. At one point there is a large, almost half-circle indentation in the shoreline, and given certain conditions it acts like a little bay or miniature cove. You may not even notice it initially, or likely even at all. This is one of those quirky features that has to be pointed out to the average Joe. In fact, given the right tidal conditions the breakers don't seem to be doing anything different in any way.

Here, the sand literally curves around just enough so that it creates a partial half-circle. Really, it's more of an indentation in the shoreline.

On certain days, however, you can walk around to the little "points" formed in the sand on either side of this pseudo bay and look back at the rest of the shoreline. You're actually looking back – eastward – at the water and shore.

If you go poking around Google Earth you can see this half circle embedded in the shoreline: it seems to be about where the 66th St. access is.

This is unusual in that most beaches have curved sections to them, but then it's primarily a kind of undulating of the shoreline – the shape wobbles as you walk up and down. Some tracts stick out a bit; some tuck inward just slightly. Here, this spot actually curves around enough to make a bay-like feature. There's no deeper water you can wade in or drop a boat in: it's really just the usual beach layout with breakers where the shoreline starts to drop off.

It's simply a curious kind of mini-bay.

The breakers here get a bit crammed as well sometimes and the wave energy does these curious things that cause all kinds of wild mini-acrobatics to happen. Waves are forced to criss-cross and thus bump into each other on the way in, sometimes sending them random directions parallel to the shore or they will jump and explode just a tiny bit.

Another fascinating surprise is that the area is often host to some plentiful agate supplies. Even in higher sand level months, when other sections of the Oregon coast are downright swimming in piles of sand, this spot can have the right kind of sand action and it opens up rocky beds.

You'll find this spot periodically – not all the time – within a half mile of the main parking lot at Roads End in Lincoln City. See the Lincoln City Virtual Tour for more photos.

Odd Fact: Where Waves Can Go the Wrong Direction

Here's a weird one very few have noticed. Waves can go the wrong direction under the right conditions.

I don't mean to be misleading: this oddity doesn't just happen in this area of Lincoln City. I've seen it near Yachats, at Manzanita, Cannon Beach and other spots. It's just that I've only been able to document it here.

If it seems to you the wave is going the wrong way, you're right. It should be coming onto shore – not outgoing. And no, the photo is not altered or flipped.

So what causes this? It's a quirky example of the science of summer on the Oregon coast.

The shot is from Lincoln City's Roads End area, taken in the summer of 2012. It's what can happen when sand levels get extremely high on the beaches, which seems to be happening more and more each summer in recent years.

The short answer: sand levels rise so high in summer they create big sand bars on the beaches, which in turn have their own little indentations. If conditions are right and the tides hit these spots just right, the gullies fill up with sea water and waves can bounce back. They get pushed back out in the direction of the sea, where they just dissipate into the next incoming wave or on the sand bar.

During summertime, sand levels always rise. Oregon coast geologist Tom Horning said it happens every year to different degrees.

"What you're seeing is just the usual, seasonal rise in beach elevation because of the summer depositing more sand," Horning said.

During winter, all that stormy wave action scours out sand. During summer, the calm wave action brings in more sand.

And then with no storm action to take it out, it just keeps building and building.

At some beaches, the sand piles up incredibly high, causing these sand bars. If you get the right combo of sand bars, low spots and the tide pounding it just right, you'll find this wacky rarity of waves coming back across the sand bar and heading the wrong way.

You can see two photos here of how this happened in Lincoln City that year.

In one shot, you can see the incoming and outgoing waves facing off against each other. In the photo at top, you see it in action.

The other interesting thing is these little wrong way-moving waves are much warmer than the incoming breakers. It feels really good, besides looking so wacky. These are tiny waves, by the way, and will not ever pose a danger. But you still need to keep an eye on sneaker waves from the usual breakers.

Where and when can you find this? It is absolutely impossible to predict. A good guess is that later in summer is your better bet, from July through September, when sand levels really have begun to do incredible things. Look for a kind of broken tidal area: giant pools of water just a bit further inland from the regular breakers, with a high spot of beach and sand between them.

You can see a moving gif of this action at https://www.beachconnection.net/news/backwave062716_722.php

Summer's high sand levels often provide other incredible sights, however. And these are easily found just about everywhere. They create a kind of faux low tide event: meaning sand levels get so high they keep the sea farther out than usual. It's as if there's an extreme low tide, but it's not.

This faux low tide can grant you much easier access to places completely dangerous or inaccessible during other times of the year. For instance, during many summers Oceanside's Maxwell Point gets such enormous sand levels that the point is almost perfectly accessible. You don't always have to go through the tunnel.

Secret Beach: NW 50th

There is, in truth, no real secret beach in Lincoln City. As one big long stretch of seven miles, unbroken by any natural feature, even the most unknown of beach accesses is fairly close to a well known one, and thus always bustling during high density days.

This one, at around NW 50th St., is about the closest you can get to a secret beach, however.

At the very northern end of town, along Logan Road and between the casino and Roads End State Recreational Site, look for the sign pointing to NW 50th amid the placid neighborhoods. Follow that to its end, where it meets NW Jetty, and you'll find a primitive gravel "driveway" which winds its way down to the beach. Along the way, there's another tunnel-like path that looks a little like the famed Hobbitt Trail near Florence (see the Upper Lane County

Virtual Tour at BeachConnection.net), although that doesn't seem to lead anywhere.

It's a gradual slope down and a truly pleasant walk beneath a thick green canopy. You are, at least for a moment, leaving the beach environment and it feels more like a stroll through the forest.

Once on this slightly clandestine beach, you'll usually discover not another soul around. Or maybe a few if it's a busy day. This is thanks to the fact it's really the only beach access in about a half mile in either direction, a true rarity in a town where all beach accesses are pretty close together.

Otherwise, it's rather unremarkable but certainly idyllic, with – like all of Lincoln City – nothing but sand and random driftwood everywhere.

There are some interesting rock features here created by a crumbling cliff.

Logan Road Back to Lincoln City - Access

To get back to other beach accesses you have to continue south on Logan Road.

Just off Logan, before the massive intersection and the strip mall, is the entrance to the Chinook Winds Casino complex. Find NW 40th there and you'll discover a tiny public beach access at its end. There's plenty of parking and decent restroom facilities.

The beach is notable for the set of three small sea stacks, which break up the view nicely if you're a photographer looking for something else to capture than just miles of sand. This is not a bad spot for agates at times, as well.

Beach Accesses off Jetty Ave. and the Semi Secret Road

At the casino, you have the option to zip back up to Highway 101 or continue on NW 40th around a tiny curve and a road that narrows enough it's barely able to hold two lanes. This leads onto Jetty Avenue and a whole host of fun beach accesses. It's quicker than driving back up to Logan, onto 101 and then down one of the side streets again.

NW Jetty Avenue features a handful of beach accesses, although the street starts and stops as it runs north and south after a few miles. But take streets like NW 40th, 39th or 26th westward from 101 and you'll find them. Other streets intersect with Jetty Ave. and take you back to the next section of the road.

Grace Hammond Access – NW 35th

Another prominent access is the Grace Hammond Access, found more or less at the bottom of NW 34th, if you take that road straight westward from the highway. There's a small parking lot, a little viewpoint with a picnic table, restroom facilities and a wheelchair-accessible ramp down to this broad, sandy beach.

It's technically part of NW 35th Place, but it's known by the name Grace Hammond, after the woman who donated the land to the state decades ago.

One of the more obvious features is the memorial to deceased dogs, a simple sign showing the names of much-loved mutts who have passed on. It's apparently maintained by the family of Ms. Hammond.

Another big feature here is that you can drive on this beach: the ramp allows some car access.

It's here where the curious beach layout of Lincoln City and Gleneden Beach begins. From this spot southward, some beaches have a rather steep slope into the tideline, which causes the waves to come rushing in rather fast and then dissipate quickly. It's often more pronounced in summer when sand levels get higher, but not always.

In this area it's rather subtle. Then the phenomenon disappears periodically as you head south down Lincoln City's expanse.

NW Jetty and NW Inlet

So far in this guide, NW Jetty has been the most westward drive, but there are moments when NW Inlet takes over that view. However, you generally won't find any beach accesses here as it's all cliffs. The hotels lining the cliffs have their own private beach entryways, however.

Suddenly, at NW 26th and NW Jetty, NW Inlet becomes the westernmost drive along the cliffs, starting with a rather stunning beach access.

Access at NW 26th

At NW 26th lies a particularly beautiful access. A small but decently-sized parking lot is surrounded by an atmospheric wall made of large stones, coming complete with bike racks. It gives the place a slight medieval castle vibe. You'll find restrooms here and a picnic table.

There are some concrete steps down to the beach – well, a lot of steps. It's not as bad it looks, however. You descend some 30 or 40 feet to this sandy spot, which is generally a nifty broad beach. One of the fascinating features is the remnants of another stony stairway which apparently was destroyed in recent decades.

Some cool rock structures lurk a little to the south, and there are occasional hints of tidepool life there.

From here, continue taking NW Jetty southward as NW Inlet is all oceanfront motels, until you reach NW 21st, where the next great big beach access is.

NW 21st Access

One of the most striking accesses is at the bottom of NW 21st (next to the Sea Horse Motel). You won't find much parking – maybe four or five spots, max. The centerpiece is that long, long….extremely long staircase. It seems endless but it's not bad heading down. Coming back up, well, let's just say it's a good thing there's a flat area or two. And hopefully you like leg cramps.

In all seriousness, it's worth it.

Parking is limited as it's squeezed between two parts of the hotel complex. The sheer length of the stairs deters some, so you may find yourself alone around here (although other accesses lurk nearby). This is a great viewpoint for whale watching or storm watching.

Odd History: Tornado Takes Out Motel

On December 14, 2010, Oregon was the recipient of a rare cluster of tornadoes in more than one place. On the same day a tornado ripped up the Aumsville area (in the Willamette Valley), the Oregon coast got hit with a double whammy of bad news. Major winds tore up a motel in Lincoln City, and on top it the Oregon Department of Fish and Wildlife (ODFW) announced a distemper outbreak in raccoons on the north coast.

Shortly before noon on that Tuesday, the tiny town of Aumsville (near Eugene) had several buildings leveled by a major twister. But a few hours before that, something large and creepy came ashore in Lincoln City, even if only fairly briefly.

Around 5 a.m., the Sea Horse Oceanfront Resort in Lincoln City got hit with a particularly nasty gust of wind that tore off some 500 feet of its roof, leaving 15 units of the motel with no covering. Debris from the roof went flying as much as two blocks away, but no objects damaged anything else nearby.

Much of the roof wound up in the overflow parking area from the Nordic Oceanfront Inn next door.

It took awhile for insurance agents and the National Weather Service to figure it out, but this indeed was no mere gust of wind: it was a small tornado.

April Christy was with the Sea Horse Oceanfront Resort at the time and was interviewed by Oregon Coast Beach Connection later that day. She said no one was in any of the 15 units, which were all oceanfront. The Sea Horse has a total of 60 units, including many vacation rentals and suites, so most of the motel was still fully operational even after the melee.

Christy said everyone knew there was a windstorm coming, but no warning it might cause this sort of damage.

"It was nothing out of the ordinary for here," Christy said that afternoon in 2010. "We think it might've been a tornado that came through."

The National Weather Service was back then quite preoccupied with the situation in Aumsville, and at first they believed it was winds from a thunderstorm. Later studies proved it was much bigger, which included some eyewitness reports from other residents of a water spout that made its way onshore.

Back then, Christy did not have an idea when the units could be repaired, or if they would.

"We don't know yet if we'll rebuild or repair," she said on that afternoon. "The insurance people are coming out tomorrow for an estimate and we'll know more."

Time, however, proved to be on their side.

"Interestingly, although the Sea Horse has 12 separate buildings and 65 rooms, we lost nary a single shingle, except for the entire roof that was launched eastward," Christy said. "One of the owners arrived early to see some debris in the parking lot and started to call Angel, one of our heavenly maintenance men, but then realized that it was much more than a broom and dustpan kind of a job."

It took some time for the owners to decide whether to replace just the roof or the entire building, but eventually the structure was razed to make way for a new one.

For a year and a half, tearing down the old building and reconstructing a new one slowly changed the face of this clifftop stretch of town. For much of that time, just a skeletal wooden structure sat where the main oceanfront building once stood. It was rather striking and surreal to see this where the building had long been.

Later, around 2012, Christy talked about what it took to create a new building in its place.

"As part of the rebuilding process, we constructed an additional floor with a roof that is super-attached," Christy said. "Thanks to our Oregon rain, it was necessary to rebuild the lodging from the foundation up. Every part of the structure is new from top to bottom, including sheetrock, rugs, and fixtures.

"A year and a half later, and over six figures in cost, the magnificent Sea Horse is better than ever."

New amenities included decks on the fourth floor and the Sea Horse's first elevator.

The Sea Horse was later sold to a different a firm, which continues operation to this day – and with a loyal following.

Midtown Area – and Odd History

Here's one moniker that simply came from modern times and not one of the tiny communities that created the whole of Lincoln City. Midtown is that area from about NW 19th down close to about NW 10th or so, which includes a whole host of businesses both historic and recent. Everything from books, ice cream, taffy, gourmet food, clothing to wacky dive bars for the nocturnally adventurous sit along here.

One of the standouts is the Bijou Theater.

Originally called the Lakeside Theater, it opened on June 3, 1937, according to the North Lincoln County Historical Museum. On the marquee that opening day was the movie Personal Property, starring Jean Harlow.

"The theater had 270 seats and movies were 35 cents for adults and 10 cents for kids," the museum writes. "The ownership changed several times and some of the Art Deco details were covered with a particle board facade. In the 1980s the theater was renamed The Bijou (French for 'Jewel') and was remodeled to have more seating and transformed back to its Art Deco roots. In 1996, the current owners, Keith and Betsy Altomare, bought the Bijou and have made great improvements to the theater's signage/marquee. Thanks to the hard work of the owners and theater goers alike, The Bijou Theater is still going strong today."

The Altomares ran into trouble around 2012 with the coming of the digital age. All new movies were moving to a digital-only format then, and that meant converting to expensive digital technology or showing only old movies thereafter. A grass roots campaign was started to fund the new machinery, and that eventually saved the day.

The theater now hosts older movies on weekend morning matinees for quite an inexpensive cover charge.

A bit of odd history in this area is the bar that currently has the giant mural of a cruise ship on the side, currently called the Cruise Inn. Back in the '90s, that building had a giant mural of an Orca to honor Keiko the Killer Whale. The whale made national headlines when he was removed from the Oregon Coast Aquarium in Newport, brought to a special air tanker in a massive, slow-moving procession where he was half-submerged, and eventually brought to the North Sea where he was released back into the wild.

Sadly, Keiko did not survive the attempts to turn him back into a wild Orca.

That mural was at least one owner back, if not more. Sometime in the early 2000s, the building became a strip joint. In a very tacky move (but conversely fairly hilariously so), the strip club painted a stripper onto the whale, straddling the poor icon in a remarkable display of bad taste.

The business apparently changed hands and by 2005 was a simple bar again, which kept the mural but adeptly 86'd the stripper. Eventually, the whale was replaced by the ship.

Odd History: Lincoln Statue

It sits on NE 22nd St., just a block or two off Highway 101: a simple depiction of a young Abe Lincoln on his horse, reading a book.

The bronze statue of Lincoln was set here in 1965, just as the town was officially formed. Sculpted by Anna Hyatt Huntington, the plaque at the bottom says it was given to the town on the condition the name never changed. However, several name changes were attempted over the years (see the previous chapter), but there's no word on what would've been done with the statue.

This steadfast art piece has a slightly amusing history.

First odd tidbit: it was Jerry Parks – owner of the Pixie Kitchen (and later Pixie Land) - who had a major hand in getting it here.

According to Ed Dreistadt, director of Lincoln City's visitor bureau Explore Lincoln City, shipping the container from the east coast was proving a major issue. It actually had to be turned around at one point because it was too high for the overpasses of 1964 American highways. So Parks and a friend drove out there and then across the country, looking for a route with no overpasses. They meandered crazily through a variety of roads, finally coming up with a passage that twisted and turned all over the place, even jutting up into Canada.

Once it arrived, it was broken in a few places, and they had to acquire a welder to repair it. It was also supposed to be facing west by the sculptor's instructions, but instead was installed incorrectly and faces north.

Secret Park: Oceanview Walk Park

Not long ago, Lincoln City gained a new park. It came into existence just as a hotel there expanded and reworked itself a bit – and the two situations are connected.

It's called Oceanview Walk Park, and if you blink you'll miss it. Look for NW 16th street, in the midtown area, then head towards the ocean. This one is a simple and quaint collection of sidewalk and bench overlooking the waves and sand. It's tiny but it's lovely.

Essentially, it was built by the Lee family that owns the Coho Oceanfront Lodge and then donated to the city, becoming part of its park system.

 You're about 100 feet or more above the surf, looking down on the soft sands of the area and a handful of rocks. It's especially engaging at night, when no one else is around and the lack of car traffic allows you to really absorb the sound of the waves. Plenty of lighting above makes the waves quite visible.

There are no beach accesses between NW 21st and NW 15th, but they're not far apart. There is only the viewpoint here above it all.

NW 15th Access and Ramp

One of the few places on the entire Oregon coast where you can drive your car is here, but within a small, restricted area. It's also about the only major tidepool spot in Lincoln City.

For this one, you can struggle to find parking space on the street – or park on the beach itself. The sands are accessed via a slightly steep ramp. But since there's a lot of loose sand here, you run the chance of getting your car stuck if you veer into the wrong place.

Restrooms sit above the whole sandy display, with a small viewpoint area that comes complete with benches and a super convenient stairway running down the side of the ramp for those pedestrians who don't feel comfortable with its incline.

From here, NW Harbor winds and turns through motel territory but dead-ends and produces no beach accesses.

Head back up to NW Inlet to continue on the back roads here.

Hidden Beach Access Near D River

You'll find this one about two blocks north of the D River and Kyllo's Restaurant, along Inlet Ave. It's tucked between two of the motels here. The pathway itself may be a secret but the nearby accesses of the D River assures that there's a lot of people here, so there's little point unless you don't feel like crossing the stream to head north.

It's technically at the end of NW 5th St. but there is no street sign.

Inlet Court Access

Just the other side of the river (or stream), on the northern face of the big restaurant at the D River, sits another tiny access that gets you onto the northern section of the D River access.

Devils Lake State Recreational Area

Head east at the traffic light at NE 6th St. to reach this favorite camping, fishing and boating spot. There are heaps of tent sites, yurt spots, paved parking and a load of other amenities in the campground. See the previous full listing.

Lincoln City Cultural Center and Visitors Information Center

If you're not looking up everything digitally, or need a real person to talk to, the info center is the place.

It, the Lincoln City Cultural Center and its gallery are all located in this historic building: the DeLake School that was built in 1926. It's also the home to the farmer's market, which is outdoors in spring, summer and early fall, then moves indoors the rest of the year.

The LCCC is a powerhouse of music and good times, hosting everything from gritty blues rock, esoteric folk, classical, jazz and a dizzying array of fusion music acts from a variety of cultures. One of its biggest events is the St. Patty's Day parties in March filled with great food and raucous Celtic rock.

540 NE Hwy 101, Lincoln City, Oregon. 541-994-9994. https://www.lincolncity-culturalcenter.org/.

D River Wayside

A big parking lot with all the facilities, viewing platforms and a sometimes-wild surf greet you here. In between, there's tons of sand and a creek for recreation. Sometimes, the city places volleyball nets on the sand so you can get your game on.

It's by far one of the most obvious spots in Lincoln City – and thus among the most crowded – but it's lovely nonetheless. To get away from the crowds, head to accesses just a bit north or south.

It has the unique distinction of varying rather wildly in width, depending on what sand levels do – and they don't always do what they're supposed to do. Even in summer, this sandy spot can suddenly get rather small. Then in winter, it can be unusually broad, but storms have been known to maraud up to the seawall and toss chunks of wood into the parking lot. Every once in awhile this hotspot actually gets closed off by state officials.

It can also be a great spot for gravel beds – and thus agates – even in summer. Geologically, it's a kooky little place.

But mostly it's a great spot for bouncing around the beach. The big kite festival fills the skies here every early summer, making quite the spectacle.

Odd Facts: D River Dispute Over World Record

Above: the D River in a state where it barely exists.

For a time in the late '90s and early 2000's, a rampant rumor raged: the D River was officially known as the shortest river in the world, but a dispute caused it to share that label with a river in Montana.

Or did it?

It's hard to say who came up with this dispute idea and when, but numerous media outlets (including myself) got sucked into the hype and publicized this.

Somewhere around 2002, I actually wrote this myself: "The D River was known as the shortest river in the world until recently. A few years ago, some grade school kids in Montana disputed this and almost won that honor for a river in their town. These days, the Guinness Book of World Records lists both rivers as shortest."

The Roe River in Great Falls, Montana supposedly had this co-honor. Even Wikipedia claims it shared that with Lincoln City for a time, "until Guinness dropped the category."

It was all over regional TV. I wasn't the only one. Somehow, we all got duped by a rumor, it seems. Or maybe there was some discussion between Lincoln City and the school kids in Montana at some point, and that made it into the news. Or perhaps there was different management at Guinness by the time I talked to them. I honestly cannot track down the original source.

All I know is around 2005 or so I contacted the Guinness folks in London to check on this and Sara Wilcox, a PR assistant with the organization, straightened me out. No, she said, there was never such a category about shortest river in the world. Or at least the Roe and the D River were never recognized for it.

If someone else decided the Roe and D Rivers should both have that honor – who knows?

The D River is indeed an oddity: there are times it is so low it doesn't even exist. Its flow can be so minute it doesn't make it under the bridge that crosses over it, and doesn't get past the Kyllo's restaurant that overlooks it. Flowing a mere 120 feet from Devil's Lake, the story goes it was allowed to remain the shortest when the Guinness folks recognized its penchant for shrinking. Depending on tidal conditions, it's not always that long.

Above, this is its normal riverbed. But this photo below from fall of 2003 shows the D River is essentially gone. There's nothing but sand where the river normally flows.

According to the North Lincoln County Historical Museum, however, the Oregon State Highway Department may have started it all decades ago (the precursor to ODOT – Oregon Department of Transportation). Though it doesn't explain the Guinness Book of World Records and Roe River story.

History of the D River's naming had something to do with its original claims.

It seems that in 1940, a newspaper contest was held to give a name to that short stream that ran from Devil's Lake to the ocean.

"Johanna Beard of Albany submitted the shortest and winning name, 'D,' " the museum wrote. "At approximately 120 feet long, D River was labeled as the shortest in the world. Many other factions disputed the 'world's shortest' claim, even prompting the Klamath County Chamber to call it a 'mere babbling brook.' "

It was the Oregon Highway Department that ended the feud by putting up signs on Highway 101 declaring "D River. World's Shortest."

An interesting side note: for decades the Sea Lion Caves near Florence claimed to have the smallest sea cave in the world. Wilcox confirmed this is indeed true: they recognize the Sea Lion Caves as just that.

"The Sea Lion Caves have a chamber 95m 310ft long, 50m 165ft wide and around 15m 50ft high in a wave cut passage 400m 1315ft long, close to Florence, on the Oregon coast, USA," she wrote in an email to me in 2005.

Odd Facts: D River Wayside's Changing Face

Every once in awhile, such as in 2011, summer's sand level changes mess with the D River in a startling way. That summer – and it's happened other times as well – the river actually shifted direction.

Normally, what is nicknamed the "world's smallest river" heads straight out to sea, with maybe a couple of small twists along the way. It's a fairly direct route.

Periodically, sand conditions on the Oregon coast during summer change that. Sometimes, it takes a long, meandering route out to sea, curving and twisting in a massive arc that takes a few hundred feet, instead of the usual 100 or so feet it takes to get to the ocean.

Jonathan Allan, with the Newport office of the Oregon Department of Geology and Mineral Industries, studies these things as a coastal geomorphologist. He described what's happening here: a situation where so much sand exists that the river course is dictated by the path of least resistance.

"Basically too much sand being transported onshore by waves, currents, and wind, when compared to the relatively low flows of the river," Allan said back in 2011. "The prevailing conditions at the moment is consistent with the summer build-up of sand, enhanced by winds which helps to transport it to the south. Since the river flows are low it is not able to maintain a normal discharge, and hence shifts in response to the build-up of the sand."

The immediate impact is a larger area with more warm water for tourists and dogs to play or wade in. Those familiar with the area will find it rather remarkable.

Canyon Drive Beach Access

It's called Canyon Drive Park, and it's one of those central Oregon coast hotspots that's not really well known. It's a bit off the beaten path, cloistered in a singular space between looming cliffside stretches that don't allow you access to the beach. It's the only gap in a mile or so radius of cliffs and neighborhoods.

So, it manages to stay a bit of a secret: a beach less traveled by the crazed throngs that can otherwise flood the other beaches in town. Usually, that is. There are times it's crammed with other beachgoers as well.

It's also hard to get to. Take SW 11th from the main stretch of Highway 101 in Lincoln City until it dead-ends at this cozy beach entrance. However, along the way the road winds, twists and turns with almost psychotic ferocity, becoming not just confusing but a little bit of a white-knuckled drive – especially if someone is walking along the last part of it, where there is no sidewalk. At this point, the road is tiny, full of blind spots, and you still have to share it with the occasional family, dog walker and / or other vehicles. If you're going 15 miles per hour on this part you may still be going too fast.

All of a sudden the landscape has turned from thick, forested neighborhood to a small beach entry, and a sizable – although not huge – view of the ocean spreads out in front of you.

Canyon Drive Park actually lies at the end of 11th and Coast Avenue – not a street called Canyon.

It's a tiny place, at least at first glance: a restroom area and a handful of parking spots is all you'll find. But it's actually part beach and part lakeside park.

Behind the restroom area sits a small grassy patch and then a small lake or pond behind that. Here, especially on lazy summer days, it's a small kick in the pants to just lounge by the lake and take in the watery reflections, the calm and the moss-covered remnants of old trees.

You'll find a little stream wandering gracefully down here, and a stone floor section of the ramp going down to the sand that adds just a little more charm to the vibe. During winters, however, this stream can get a bit more frenzied.

The beach itself is typical of Lincoln City: plenty of soothing sands and a tideline than can dip rather steeply sometimes, causing the waves to crash just a little louder than a more steadily sloped beach.

Because of the ramp it is wheelchair accessible.

To the north, it's about a mile to the next beach access: at the D River area. To the south: it's also about a mile to the next one, in the Nelscott District, at around SW 32nd Street.

Lincoln City Outlets Mall

A massive shoppers' paradise by any standards, but if you're not into dealing with the throngs – at any time of year – then stick to the beaches. It's found on Highway 101 near SW 12 St. Really, you can't miss it. (541) 996-5000.

Agnes Creek Green Space and Trail

If you're on Highway 101, or you've just begun to go south on SW Coast Ave., you'll see a lot of trees for a good mile or two. This is a forest within a coastal resort town: the Agnes

Creek Green Space. It's unbroken except by SW Bard Rd, which meets up with SW Coast Ave. from Highway 101 just south of SW 17th St., via a long, winding and twisting – and purely gravel - road.

There's over two miles of hiking trail here, meandering through this thick greenery overhead and featuring all kinds of wildlife. The trailhead is about halfway through the open space with parking on either side of the road.

Clifftop Drive Along SW Anchor

Along SW Coast, there are no public beach accesses. Some resort hotels and rental homes have their own switchbacking stairways down the cliff, however. It eventually turns into SW Anchor.

There is, however, a stunning but simple gravel pullout or two where you can gaze out over the cliffs and down to the beach below. It is not an official viewpoint, but it doesn't appear to be big enough to become private property so it's likely not going anywhere.

It's an extremely pleasant clifftop drive around here, with various ocean vistas popping up now and then between the homes and sections of treeline. It's suggested you take your time and take in the view.

Nelscott District

The first beach access you'll encounter (a mile south of the Canyon Drive access) is SW 33rd Ave. Anything north of that is either clifftop homes (or along Highway 101 you're on the eastern face of the forest lands of the Agnes Creek Open Space).

After you've gone through that forested stretch, you're in the old Nelscott district, a charming and comely little place that was once an unincorporated village all its own. The Nelscott area lies just north of the enormous Inn at Spanish Head, including a large bluff that's been turned into a winding street full of beautiful homes.

A smattering of shops, eateries, the Theater West playhouse and other goodies sit astride 101.

The area was co-founded by Charles Nelson and his son Earl, who opened the Lincoln Book Shop there in 1936, according to the local history museum. A surf shop now occupies that building.

Curious History: WW2 Submarine Lookout - Motel Life

Two curious bits of Lincoln City history are tied together here in Nelscott: the odd and awkward ways of tourism a century ago and the remnants of World War 2 in the area.

The early 1940s were a darker time for the Oregon coast. Considered almost open bait for an invasion, it - like the rest of the west coast - was on high alert for incoming ships, aircraft or submarines from the Japanese. This was also a time of rations, hardships, and a tourism industry that had been stopped in its tracks. (Above: what the "Submarine House" looks like right now.)

One historic home in Lincoln City sat perched on the cliffs of the Nelscott district during World War II and kept an eye on the seas. Now called the "Submarine," it's a vacation rental home provided by A1 Beach Rentals.

Its brief but interesting history is intertwined with the growth of tourism in the proto-Lincoln City.

Throughout the early century, the little villages along this seven-mile stretch were starting to build a real tourism industry, especially Nelscott (which currently includes hotspots like the Inn at Spanish Head, The Christmas Village shop and the SW 35th access). A handful of hotels and little resorts sprang up around here in the '20s and '30s, yet most kinds of tourist lodgings were still simple tents. These had no running water nor places to bathe. Most villages, like Oceanside, Cannon Beach and Seaside, had special facilities where you had to pay to use the restroom or take a shower.

Yuck.

In the early '20s and '30s, this area became a haven for writers, attracted by that local bookshop built by Earl Nelson. It also featured the precursor to the modern motel: what was called the Nelscott Auto Park. This had evolved from a tent camp, where tents were transitioned to little shacks – and then to cabins – where you could park your car next to where you stayed.

By the late '30s, even the auto park model decayed in popularity, being replaced by the idea of motels. By 1940, the State Parks system had begun to build even more of a tourism industry for the future Lincoln City area. But in 1942, the Japanese bombing of Pearl Harbor killed just about any tourism growth, and these little villages – like the rest of the western coastline – were subject to blackouts at night and of course gas rations. The latter really ended tourism.

In the tiny unincorporated village of Nelscott, something interesting was about to happen that would leave an intriguing remnant of World War II Oregon coast.

The Nelscott home now known as the "Submarine" vacation rental was built around 1940. Originally, the house was built on property bequeathed to a talk radio host from San Francisco by a woman who died in 1940 or so. Confined to a nursing home, she was a faithful listener of his in the 1930s. When she passed on and gave him a large portion of the lot, it was on the condition that he build his own house there.

About that time, the talk show host left California for the Oregon coast and the slowly-burgeoning tourist area that was then called Nelscott. Two short years after the man acquired the property, the Japanese pulled the U.S. into the war and that ended all hopes of any flood of travelers and the hospitality industry that we're all used to today.

New construction completely stalled, and soon troops began filling these little coastal towns. It was in those early years of the war that the talk show host rented his large home out to the military. They set up the observation posts there, with the mission of scanning the seas for any sign of Japanese or German craft, especially submarines. It was thus nicknamed the "Submarine House" by its military tenants. Currently on Anchor Street, at the time it was called Marview Avenue.

According to A1 Beach Rentals, a large gun emplacement was built on the south side of the building, where the fence ends at the abrupt cliff. Apparently, erosion eventually took away that part in later years. The gun reportedly fell over the edge one day.

Why no pictures of this bit of Oregon coast WWII history?

Back in 2016, Anne Hall was head of the North Lincoln County History Museum in Lincoln City. She said pictures of anything to do with war operations were not allowed.

"So, we don't have anything but a few pictures of troops and some other buildings until just after the war," Hall said.

Consequently, she said none of the information provided to Oregon Coast Beach Connection by A1 or the homes' owners can be verified. And there is no way to tell what the actual lookout stations looked like at the time.

One thing is known: as the Great War went on, it became clearer that the West Coast was not going to get invaded. Troops began filtering out of the Nelscott area long before V Day came.

However, once the post-war economic boom began, tourism along the length of the Oregon coast exploded. And so Nelscott itself expanded as well.

Hall said the Koski family (already early homesteaders in the area) bought up the "Submarine Lookout" house sometime in the 1950s, and they owned it until about 1978. It was then segmented into separate apartments, and in the early '80s the decking and hot tub were added. It's been a vacation rental home ever since.

The boys in uniform missed out on that relaxing fun by 40 years.

You won't see any submarines from the home, but it is situated almost directly in front of the famed Nelscott Reef, which sits a couple miles offshore and attracts gobs of surfers almost year-round. It's also a great vantage point to spot whales. The home features a whopping 90 steps down the cliff to the beach, but there are benches along the way.

Called the "Submarine" on A1 Beach Rentals' website, it's often paired with the adjoining Anchor house. See www.a1beachrentals.com.

Another Wild WWII Tale: there was a local military commander who threatened martial law in the area that would later become Lincoln City. According to a newspaper clipping provided by the history museum, one of the generals in charge of this area during wartime wrote an op-ed scolding locals for not obeying blackouts at night. They had sent patrols up and down central coast waters and found the little villages of Taft, Nelscott, Cutler City and so on mostly non-compliant. He warned he might impose martial law if they didn't cut out light sources after dark.

Crazy History: Storm Damages Balcony

Storms come and go on the Oregon coast, and some make for more attention than others. On January 21, 2017, a storm did something at least one local firefighter had never seen before: smashed an upstairs balcony.

That particular storm sent massive surges into places they didn't normally go.

On that Saturday, the National Weather Service (NWS) in Portland had issued a variety of beach alerts, warning of serious dangers on the beaches. Lincoln City can be especially treacherous as its beaches are not very broad. That day, buoys out at sea documented 20-foot waves, living up to the surf warnings. At the time they said actual breakers hitting the beaches could be much higher, and that's exactly what happened.

Later estimates said they could've been 40-foot waves hitting the beaches.

Near the Surftides in Lincoln City hotel complex, rescue crews responded to a vacation rental around 8 a.m. with reports of a woman hanging from an upstairs balcony. At the time, Captain Jim Kusz, with North Lincoln County Fire and Rescue, said a massive wave that appeared to be about 12 to 15 feet high slammed the second story deck she was standing on while watching the storm. The deck was almost completely demolished, dumping furniture and a barbecue onto the beach below.

Kusz said the wave was seen on hotel surveillance later, which caused him to update his initial estimation of the wave from 10 feet to as much as 15 feet.

Witnesses heard the 45-year-old woman screaming and saw her hanging from a hot tub. She was pulled up by her husband. The woman was taken by ambulance to the hospital and treated for minor injuries.

Many officials on the Oregon coast, including Kusz, were saying this is a first: while wave damage to homes and other structures happens occasionally, no one can remember hearing of someone actually being hurt while on a balcony.

"This [kind of storm] is extremely rare," Kusz said. "I've been here for 22 years and have never heard of someone being hurt like this."

The neighboring Surftides hotel also sustained some damage. Kusz said it's quite possible a large log was in the waves and smacked the properties.

Later that same day, at approximately 11:15 a.m., a 65-year-old Lincoln City woman was struck by a "sneaker wave" while walking on the beach near Mo's Restaurant on Siletz Bay. She sustained an injured ankle and was also taken to the hospital.

At the time, Kusz urged the public to keep off the beaches and far back from areas where waves were hitting.

"Don't walk on beaches during these high surf advisories," Kusz said in an interview with me for Oregon Coast Beach Connection back then.

It's such an understated way to put it, considering the circumstances.

As a side note: more oceanic carnage happened in Rockaway Beach that same day. There, several condo units were destroyed by massive waves that came over the bluffs, even damaging cars in a parking lot. One condo unit had an enormous surge come through one end and shove furnishings around so hard it caused a garage door to bulge on the other side of the building.

Another surge came through a parking lot and pushed several cars into each other. Luckily, no one was hurt in Rockaway Beach.

About a year later, in January of 2018, also in Lincoln City, more major storm damage happened. This time, both the Sea Gypsy Rentals and the Sandcastle Motel were hit by waves, along with Kyllo's Restaurant. The Sandcastle and other buildings were evacuated, while the Sea Gypsy experienced a massive wave punching through one of the units, knocking over a woman in her 70s. She was taken to the hospital and released, later describing her ordeal on regional television stations.

Kyllo's, next to the Sea Gypsy, had a natural gas pipe severed by waves and debris and it too was evacuated. Damages in that storm overall were estimated at over one million dollars.

 If you need more reasons to heed these storm warnings, that same day a man met his maker at Depoe Bay by venturing too close to the waves on those rocky stretches. He climbed over the sea wall of the downtown area – and for some crazy reason – thought it would be okay to get a better look at the mammoth waves that were already twice the height of humans. He was swept into the ocean and his body was never found.

SW 33rd St. Access

Head down SW 32nd or SW 35th to find this.

A tiny, nondescript access with minimal parking, a water fountain and a handicapped-accessible ramp doesn't seem like much at first glance. It sits on a small back road, far from just about everything, and sure, there's a picnic bench and a lovely view of the ocean. But it's the last access for awhile – quite awhile – if you're walking north, a spot you may be thankful for if you're hoping to reduce the leg cramps from walking along that desolate mile where only soaring cliffs occupy the view to the east.

This place is the key to a couple of astounding things: some great wave action in winter and the closest access to some large bulbous rock formations that help fuel the fun finds of agates in Lincoln City.

During storm season, this place can get dangerous and waves (which include the large objects in them) can come jumping over the sea wall and flood the area. Every once in awhile, winter storms result in the picnic table getting smashed to bits.

This is an entertaining and fairly safe spot at night, with a little bit of lighting to guide you around the beach at first, but then it fades as you walk northward – which may allow you to see that famed glowing sand phenomenon.

SW 35th Access

This one is unique in a number of ways. Take a turn west on SW 32nd St. and you'll find it just to the north, or simply head down SW 35th St. A tiny parking lot with restrooms and a small set of steps down to the cushy, thick sand, this is where the tideline can get quite steep and result in raucous waves that crash in hard and fast, but then dissipate into timid little lines of white foam. It takes a bit of getting used to, actually.

It's usually more pronounced in winter, but summer can pile the tufts of sand high enough that it has this somewhat startling effect as well.

A few hundred feet to the south you'll find some fun rock structures for climbing (at acceptably lower tides, that is) and the beach below the Inn at Spanish Head.

There's something especially calming about this stretch of strand. Perhaps it's the relatively low density of people you often find, or maybe there's just some mysterious vibe to the spot.

This is the last public access for about a half mile until you reach the Siletz Bay.

It's also where you'll find a slightly mysterious statue of a sea lion, and a plaque explaining some of its story. This is one fascinating and ultra cute little tale of history, however.

Odd History: Joe the Sea Lion

For about about a week or two in the early 1930s, the area that would eventually be known as Lincoln City had a kind of sea lion mascot and a sizable claim to fame. The big barking beast brought thousands to the tiny Oregon coast hamlet, a major feat at the time as these beaches hardly saw that kind of traffic back then. Indeed, Highway 101 wasn't even completely finished.

The little village of Nelscott was one of seven that would incorporate into Lincoln City in the early '60s, but back then it was a beachy backwater place during the pre-war years that barely had paved roads. Yet for a brief time it had Joe the Sea Lion - as someone named him - who briefly became an honorary citizen and a major tourist attraction, before such things existed on the central coast.

The result of Joe's brief time there was a wacky tale of human-sea lion diplomacy, goofy behavior, major publicity and then even, sadly, an ugly act of jealousy.

Photo of Joe the Sea Lion Courtesy North Lincoln County Historical Museum

According to documents from the North Lincoln County Historical Museum, it all started in the last week of March – in 1936 or 1933. Written testaments disagree on that.

One document attests it was a "battle-scarred male sea lion," found on the beach by a man named Dave Dewey. It was presumed the sea lion was looking for a cave to recuperate in.

The document goes on: "He [was] lassoed by him and brought up the ramp and into our town. A fenced-in place was built for him, but every night he would escape and by morning enter the first open door. (He must have mistaken it for the entrance of the cave.)"

That's when it gets hilarious. Residents recounted how he would "be discovered in one of the waterfront houses, much to the alarm of the residents who were obliged to show him out."

Another document talks of Joe actually making his way over picket fences, and either being found in the house or on the porch. It even pointed out he managed to not crush flowerpots or gardens. But Joe the Sea Lion certainly scared those inside.

This was apparently his morning routine: he would bust out of his wire pen and then look for a home to crash.

In an interview with Oregon Coast Beach Connection in 2016, Anne Hall, curator of the museum back then, said he was also known for heading out into the ocean to catch his own fish. Apparently, however, he would not eat what humans tried to give him. She added he did become quite friendly and close to the humans, and did not appear to show aggression towards them.

In fact, there was one notoriously hilarious interaction between people and beast: "during his residence ashore he had become fond of his captors and loved being bathed with a hose and having his back rubbed with a broom," one resident wrote.

Exactly how long he was around is unclear, according to Hall. Locals seem to indicate it wasn't much more than a week in the documents, but Hall believes it was a bit longer.

Joe the Sea Lion was there long enough to grab some serious time in the spotlight. The Oregonian wrote about him and suddenly the little town had over 5,000 visitors in a week or less. He was, by the standards of the time, bigger than Keiko the Killer Whale was at Oregon Coast Aquarium in the '90s.

"Traffic was so intense that the streets had to be re-graveled," one local wrote.

Then, some sad and petty jealousy took over. The residents of nearby Taft – now the very southern end of Lincoln City – felt upstaged. Although in the end, it was indeed for the better for this wild animal.

One document reads: "He probably would have accepted our hospitality for some time had not a small group of people in another resort town became jealous of the publicity we were getting and complained to the game warden who came in a truck, loaded Joe into it, dumped him into the surf and forced him to swim away from our shores."

Another telling has Joe the Sea Lion complaining vigorously as he's put aboard that truck. It says "Joe complained every foot of the way." Then officials chased him back into the ocean and made sure he swam away.

Other reports show Joe actually came back briefly. He loved it here. Officials dragged him out again and returned him to the wild once more.

Years later, one of the Oregon coast's first major tourist attractions - Sea Lion Caves near Florence – apparently found him. A dead sea lion was discovered there, and it's believed to be Joe as the body had the "same deep battle scar in his neck and shoulder and was blind in one eye."

You can find more Lincoln City history at the North Lincoln County History Museum, 4907 SW Hwy 101, Lincoln City, Oregon. (541) 996-6614.

History: Constructing the Inn at Spanish Head

Historical photo courtesy North Lincoln County Historical Museum

Those hillsides on the Oregon coast overlooking the sands aren't always the most stable of places. Still, one hotel icon of the area managed to plop itself in just such a place with stellar success.

It started with a bit of wheeling and dealing, and ended in a business model that's still a little cutting edge today: apparently the first condominium-style hotel in all of Oregon.

Lincoln City's Inn at Spanish Head hotel now sits as a 10-story-high hotel, what would be by far the tallest structure on the coast if it were entirely above ground. But only two stories are visible from the highway. Everything about it is oceanfront: from the restaurant, the lobby, the rooms to even the ladies restroom in the diner.

How it came to be, with its varied twists, turns and architectural challenges, is an interesting story. Starting with the historical photographs of its construction. (It's interesting to note that the giant condo building in Seaside is the tallest non-lighthouse construct on the coast).

The photos are rather awe-inspiring - a bit like watching real life Transformer robots moving on the beaches of the Oregon coast. They're a bit surreal.

The Inn's beginnings even have a small tie to the beach bill that allowed Oregon's beaches to be public.

Initially, the Inn at Spanish Head was the brainchild of a tax court judge. In the '60s, a Salem man named Peter Gunnar had been a lawyer and then a judge in the State Tax Court. He bought up a piece of property in Lincoln City, about 500 feet of a beachfront cliff, with no particular idea in mind. An article in the Statesman Journal in 1969 (then called the Capital Journal) said he simply thought it would be a good investment.

The article goes on:

"Later he visited Hawaii and there became interested in the condominium resort hotel idea - a plan in which unit owners rent their space to others while they don't occupy it themselves. The units usually are sold as an investment and a second home."

It was here that the company Condominiums Northwest, Inc. began. This company later started not just the Inn at Spanish Head but also some other high-profile resorts.

Gunnar had gone from tax law expert to developer. Somehow, Gunnar suddenly became enamored of the world of hotels, and even later co-authored a book on the hospitality industry.

In order to get state permission, he had to do a bit of wheeling and dealing, however. The Oregonian reported in 1967 that Gunnar deeded 1.1 acres of beach land to the state for public use, right about the time the beach bill was being put into place. This opened the door to permits for the hotel.

Gunnar came up with the Spanish/Mediterranean design theme, partially for the technical reasons that were demanded by building a structure ten stories up from a cliff face. It needed a certain degree of strength, which could best be achieved by pouring concrete. But at the time, Oregonians fancied logs and lumber for their vacation resorts.

So to tie together the technical needs and the aesthetic requirements to market the hotel, Gunnar targeted Oregon's connections to Spain. He researched the historical and cultural influence of Spain on this state and found quite a few to play on.

"This influence became the impetus for the design with a red tile roof, arches and concrete structure," said Susan Burr, who was general manager of the Inn at Spanish Head in 2015. "Original interior design was to be a Mediterranean theme."

Construction of the inn began on April 26, 1968. The first concrete was poured on July 9, and some 7,100 cubic yards of concrete followed throughout the project. 408 tons of steel were used.

Architect was Donald Richardson from Salem. Geologists they employed for a soil analysis showed a solid rock base beneath the planned project. This was half the battle for a sturdy structure on a hillside like this.

"The Oregon Beach Law enacted in 1967 required the initial design of the Inn be adjusted to bring the building behind the 16-foot line (16 feet above mean high water)" Burr said.

Units went quickly, with all of them pre-sold prior to its opening for the owners on October 25, 1969.

"Remarkably fast construction to me for a 10-story concrete building built down the face of an oceanfront cliff on the Oregon coast, in a small town," Burr said.

On December 6 of that year it opened to the public.

That official opening featured Oregon Congressman Wendall Wyatt as a speaker, and Governor Tom McCall was there to formally accept the beach area's deed that was part of the original deal two years prior.

Another interesting feature is the tunnel going under the highway to the parking lot – something definitely out of the ordinary for an Oregon coast hotel.

A little while later, Inn of the Seventh Mountain in Bend and the Inn at Otter Crest, just down the road near Depoe Bay, were the next two developments of Condominiums Northwest, Inc. That firm went bankrupt eventually, leaving all properties in other hands at various points in the last 40 years.

Now, you can't really go anywhere in this soaring Oregon coast landmark without seeing the ocean. Burr admits the view from the ladies' restroom is often a surprise to folks.

Despite all the technological changes since the genesis of the Inn (there were no electronic key cards or satellite TV then), the vision has largely stayed the same. It's managed to thrive all these decades, sitting on that base of Gunnar's original ideas – one that's about as firm as the foundation of basalt the hotel was carved into.

Still, even Burr sometimes wonders what made Gunnar plunge into being a hotelier after years of practicing tax code law.

"Seems like once he got started on the resort condo idea he really went with it," Burr said.

North Lincoln County Historical Museum

Everything you ever wanted to know about Lincoln City's past, including artifacts from local native tribes, pioneers and old photos as well as a collection of glass floats. It also hosts numerous lectures and events that are particularly interesting. 4907 Highway 101. (541) 996-6614. www.northlincolncountyhistoricalmuseum.org/

Overlook Park

There's a secret viewpoint lying along the northern edge of the Taft neighborhood in Lincoln City. It sits at the end of a suburban street (namely Beach Ave.), featuring this incredible viewpoint of Siletz Bay and a bench at the edge of this cliff.

This place is called Beach Ave. Overlook Park. Here, you're directly above the bend where the cliffs turn from the bayside to the beaches. It is a bit of a hidden spot and highly underutilized.

There's not much to it: a simply grassy spot with the bench tucked away between a wind-tossed set of bushes. Oh, but oh the view. It's an enchanting place to sit and contemplate the oceanic drama below.

Odd History: Redhead Roundup

History is dotted with all sorts of things we wouldn't exactly do today.

On the borderline of that is a somewhat cringe-inducing yet amusing bit of trivia regarding a yearly event which took place on the central Oregon coast: the Redhead Roundup. It was a kind of beauty contest that actually honored red-haired women. And it did at least honor all body types, though its approach would be considered tacky today.

By and large the Redhead Roundup was harmless and really kind of funny now.

According to the North Lincoln County Historical Museum, the Redhead Roundup was started by Taft resident and businessman Manville Robison in 1931, who owned a popular restaurant at the time called the Green Anchor in the tiny village.

It quickly gained in popularity, and within a few short years it had become a full two-day summer festival, bringing in some 25,000 visitors at times. In 1935, it attracted 15,000 people.

The focus was, however, the girls. Museum curator Jeff Syrop wrote: "There were also contests for beauty, reddest hair, plumpest redhead, longest red hair, and more. The only stipulation to participate was that you had to have natural red hair."

Syrop said that women from other states showed up to be a part of the event.

Still, it soon attached other attractions, such as rides, parades, dances, and games. It was known to create massive traffic jams through tiny Taft. This was back when Highway 101 had just been built, but even then most of the streets in Taft were still gravel.

It only lasted ten years, however. Syrop said: "The last Redhead Roundup was in 1941 when WWII brought gas rationing and a 'no large crowds during war' policy."

After the war, there were several attempts to bring back the festival throughout the decades, but none of them were a success. The idea is dead today.

Taft and Siletz Bay

Above: a somewhat historical photo of Taft from the '90s. This unique, massive chunk of driftwood was rather famous for awhile until it washed away in the early 2000s.

Head down that big hill just after the Inn at Spanish Head hotel complex and you're entering Taft. It's probably the most unique and quirky of the neighborhoods of Lincoln City, with a vibrant nightlife scene that can be a bit startling to the uninitiated. Those who enjoy that kind of dive bar scene love the area, however.

The area is one of several sections of the city that were originally a separate tiny town (see How Lincoln City was Formed).

Taft is a charming little place to go wandering – either on the beach or along the business district. A funky-colored surf shop sits nearby, as well as coffee shops, pizza joints, gourmet hamburgers and some delicious ethnic surprises. It's yummy and generally quite creative.

Odd Facts: Colored Rocks at the Bend

As you round the bend from Siletz Bay to the beaches of Lincoln City, some unique objects may present themselves just beneath the waves. It's rarely seen, and it will depend greatly on how far the tide is out and how low sand levels have become. It's a puzzling yet wondrous sight.

Brightly colored rocky shelves sometimes show up in this section of Lincoln City. And they're not just bright colors – they're unusual forms of greens and reds. They're like streaks in these intertidal slabs, appearing in a way that's almost crystal-like. As if you might be able to see through them. But you can't. They're simply either sea life that's clinging to these rocks or they could be veins of rock material that help create the agates you find in the area.

There is one such jasper vein near the SW 35th St. access, buried deep beneath the sands.

Jennifer Sears Glass Art Studio

The famed spot where you can blow your own glass piece, it's been a fascinating attraction for years. You can also just sit and watch the art pieces being created. If you create your own, it must cool overnight and then it can be picked up – or shipped. Keep that in mind if you intend on making your own masterwork. Appointments are necessary.

Otherwise known as the Lincoln City Glass Center, it was originally named after Jennifer Sears, the director of the Lincoln City Visitors Bureau in the '90s and early 2000s, until she passed away. She was the one who actually implemented the Finders Keepers glass float balls promotion that runs almost all year. 4821 SW Hwy 101. Lincoln City, Oregon. 541-996-2569. https://www.lincolncityglasscenter.com/

History: The Pines Hotel, The Pines Bar

These days, there's only a parking lot there in Taft, though you'll still see a sign declaring The Pines Restaurant and Lounge. Almost directly across the street from the bar called Snug Harbor, you'll see only concrete. Yet a decade ago there was a wild 'n crazy bar called The Pines, and before that a famed hotel.

According to the North Lincoln County Historical Museum, The Pines Hotel was originally built in 1927 by Fred Watson for what was then gobs of money: $20,000. It was the first upscale resort hotel for Taft, hosting a ballroom, a restaurant, and it was a popular place for locals to play cards and gamble.

About a block or two to the north, there was a peewee golf course and hamburger stand. There were also speakeasy's around here and the occasional brothel over the years. Taft was pretty wild in its early days.

The hotel burned down in 1976, however. It was rebuilt, but by the late '90s had fallen into a state of disrepair, and by the early 2000s the bar known as The Pines Restaurant and Bar was the primary biz there. The eatery portion had a decent enough reputation, though it was greasy spoon fare for its last decade or so. Breakfasts were certainly hearty and copious.

The boozy side of the operation was a bizarre dive bar by any stretch of the imagination, and it was on the rough side. Even Portland connoisseurs of wacky dive bars were a bit scared by it. The place seemed an endless parade of strange and hilarious moments taking place one after another. It wasn't uncommon to see one or two elderly patrons passed out at any one time, and while most locals were the awesome and quirky friendly-types that Taft is known for, this goofy locale had a few bad apples here and there.

Still, the place provided plenty of memories for the adventurous.

However, it too burned down in 2008, leaving only that empty lot. The remaining sign may be confusing to those who have no clue what it was – or certainly what they missed – but it's a pleasant reminder of recent history to those who were there.

Siletz Bay

All this is accessible by SW 51st St., just before you leave Lincoln City, if you're heading southward.

It's here where they hold the famed sandcastle festival every year, and it's here you'll find by far the most driftwood in town, perhaps on all of the Oregon coast (except for maybe one part of Rockaway Beach). Chunks of formerly floating wood are crammed together here in a way they are nowhere else on these shores. It can actually be a little difficult to move.

It's easier to walk right along the shore or along the backside of the beach up against the brushy hills, if you don't want to step over all the large masses of wood.

The pier is in this spot, allowing you to walk out and gaze over the scenic pleasantries of softly lapping waves.

Insider Tip: head to the pier at night and you'll love the solitude and the ultra-soothing sounds of those unusually calm waves. All of it under the stars. Or maybe you'll be lucky enough to see fog banks drifting through the night air, illuminated by street lamps or the neon glow of one of the big electric signs.

Sometimes as you're gazing out into the soft splash of this mesmerizing bay, you might see little heads bobbing up and down in the water – watching you. Yes, sometimes the wildlife here checks out the humans.

Seals and sea lions like to haul out on the edge of the Salishan Spit across the bay here – mostly harbor seals. You can see gobs of the slovenly creatures lounging around the sand on the other side and sometimes even hear them barking and carrying on.

At times, they frolic in the water, splashing and diving and flopping around again in the current. It's then when you might spot one looking back at you.

Siletz Bay is a lot bigger than people think. The most obvious part of it is that section bordered by the small island of rocks, the pier and to the south by the tip of the Salishan Spit on the other side of the bay. Indeed, it just keeps on going for awhile alongside the highway, really going for at least a couple of miles. Along the way, there's bundles of hidden stuff – or at least stuff that people just don't seem to know about. That includes a massive wildlife refuge, another secret park, and a failed community develop that was supposed to be the hottest, hippest place to live on the coast.

Every 4th of July, Taft is the center of attention on the coast, with an enormous fireworks display going on down the beach a ways. During the day, as everyone stakes out their spot on the beach, this area is a hub of activity. The nearby bars are usually packed with tourists in one heck of a party mood. This is some of the best fun you can have on Independence Day anywhere.

What's In a Name: Siletz. According to the local history museum, the Siletz Indian Reservation was created in 1856. This housed some 26 different bands of native peoples, displaced because the U.S. government was making way for gold miners who decided they should have free reign over the lands the locals already lived on.

The name Siletz has two possible origins. One is that it comes from a Rogue tribal name of "silis," which means "black bear." Another is that it comes from the natives' word "Se-La-Gees," which means "crooked rope" and apparently was used to describe the many bends in the river.

Odd History: Mysterious Shipwreck and Its Legends

The Ghost Ship. There have long been legends here of a ghost ship that appears in Siletz Bay, poking briefly out of a fog bank and then disappearing again. These paranormal legends have gone on for generations. There was even a documentary made around 2000 about the ghost tales of Lincoln City which contained some purported witnesses to these spooky sights.

Even stranger: there is a ghost of a shipwreck here. A large sailing ship crashed in these waters more than 150 years ago and parts of it managed to lodge in the middle of the bay for a long time. Then chunks of it disappeared in the mid-century, however.

Shipwreck of the Blanco. Buried in the mud and muck of the bay is a brig named the Blanco, which wrecked – presumably – sometime in 1864. It was bound for Coos Bay after leaving San Francisco late that year, but it was another year before a newspaper story in Salem recounted the wreckage in the bay. The masts were gone and its hull was essentially split in two. Its cargo vanished.

Its crew were missing as well.

There are not even really legends about what happened to them. It's possible some local tribesmen might have killed them for their goods: some natives around the time were seen with clothing and equipment clearly salvaged from the wreckage in one way or the other. What local tribes are left on the central Oregon coast are not usually direct descendants of the indigenous peoples at the time because of forced movement elsewhere. More than likely the crew were killed in the wreck mishap itself.

What happened to the ship after its skeleton sank is a bit of a mystery still to this day. Its remains have popped up now and again, but apparently not since the '80s or even earlier. There are a handful of photographs of it, mostly from the '50s and '60s.

There's a plot twist here, however: the wreck may not be the Blanco. In fact, apparently the only documentation saying it was so came from that newspaper article. Historians in the area say whatever wreck is in the bay could be a number of different vessels that met their doom along the central coast.

In 2005, a group of scientists from various places around the Pacific Northwest used magnetometry to poke around the bay at spring's extreme low tides, utilizing a cart filled with science equipment to look into the mud flats. According to articles by the L.A Times and the Newport News-Times in the mid 2000s, the group came here at the behest of Sandy Pfaff in 2004, who was the head of the Lincoln City Visitors Bureau back then.

They first conducted interviews with those who had seen it poke its withered bones out of the bay over the mid and early 20th century, but wound up with conflicting locations. With the photos, they were able to somewhat narrow the search grid. The cart full of gear – dubbed Beachcomber 1 – did its little number on the sand and mud in 2005, and the data took another two years to analyze.

In the end, results were not totally conclusive, but there was a mass of something buried beneath the bay that was about the right shape and size of a ship like the Blanco. The object even matched the orientation, based on the old photographs. Bradley Matson, a Beaverton geophysicist, was one of the scientists working on the project, and he said that while not for certain it was fairly likely this was the old Blanco.

The visitors bureau had hopes they might be able to dig it up and then display it at the history museum. Pfaff told the News-Times in 2008 that the idea was tabled indefinitely because of the economy at the time and what would be intense negotiations with the government over such a project.

Siletz Bay Park and the Refuge

Look for it just a tiny bit south of the 51st Ave entrance to Siletz Bay.

This small parking lot – and another viewing area next to it – both look out over the Siletz Bay. Information kiosks and other facilities are found here, and just a short walk away sits the big pier jutting out into the bay. It's an engaging spot for a picnic and there are restrooms.

You can walk over the Siletz River bridge to see more of the bay and those funky rock structures up close, or head down the road less than half a mile and you'll come to some more pullouts where photographing is, well, picture perfect.

As you wander south away from Lincoln City, just past the Siletz Bay, it seems there is much more Siletz Bay along the route. It's difficult to notice as you zoom over the bridges and passing lanes, with marshland on both sides of the highway, but the bay runs along much of that – in the distance.

You're now entering the Siletz Bay National Wildlife Refuge, and a host of interesting features no one knows about.

The refuge encompasses about two miles from north to south, an area of land and marshes. Sections of varying widths are on either side of Highway 101. It begins a ways east of SW 51st and ends just a tad south of a tributary of the Siletz River. A total of 568 acres create this wonder.

After you've passed over the main Siletz River, keep an eye out for Millport Slough Lane on the eastern side of the highway. This small road leads you to the parking lot for the trails and the boat launches that allow you access to the many natural facets of the refuge.

This place is teeming with life and fun activities, although in order to see much of it you need a canoe or kayak. It is, after all, a wildlife refuge made of marshes and thus human interaction is to be at a minimum. Some seasonal waterfowl hunting is allowed, however, but taking in the scenery, photography and some seasonal fishing are the primary means of having a ball here.

The majority of it is tidal salt marsh, covered in eel grass and hosting a huge variety of birds, fish and even some Roosevelt elk (which you mostly only see up around the north coast).

Alder Island is one small section you can walk around on, and lucky for you there's the recently-installed Alder Island Nature Trail. It's a shorty, but a goodie.
https://www.fws.gov/refuge/siletz_bay/. 541-867-4550.

Siletz River and Kernville

The Siletz River is the sizable body of water that feeds into the bay, meandering through the marshes, forests and hills for tens of miles until it all meets up with the tiny town of Siletz and eventually Toledo, near Newport. Running alongside it the whole time is smallish Highway 229, faithfully following the river.

Close to the Highway 101 and Highway 229 junction is teeny, tiny Kernville, surprisingly the first community developed here in the 1800s. Really, it's only a smattering of buildings, the most prominent of which is the old restaurant seen from the highway. This was for a number of years the Kernville Steakhouse until around 2010 or so. It's notable because the building that was there before the restaurant was featured in the 1971 film "Sometimes a Great Notion."

Odd Facts: Siletz Keys and Dead Trees

Two quirky features of the area lurk around here as well. One is a vague remnant of a failed community development and the other a slightly spooky sight.

Directly across from the Millford Slough Lane, on the western side of the highway, is a small road darting off that direction called Keys Place. At its end are a small smattering of homes somewhat informally called Siletz Keys. This was part of a hip and cool new development by that name which was meant to be much bigger, but it failed.

Probably intended to be a kind of elite neighborhood, Siletz Keys even had advertising cards featuring a girl in a bikini touting how exciting and awesome this new community would be. An area about three or more times the size of the current development was slated for construction, but the bulk of the land was quickly deemed too watery – high water tables were among the issues. There were also problems keeping the tidal marshes and waters of the Siletz Bay out, so huge dump trucks came in and poured more landfill into the area to shore it up.

Not only did that not work, but it caused the estuary waters to change in directions and strength in the 1960s, which suddenly increased erosion along the Salishan Spit. It went from 573 feet wide in the 1870s to about 171 feet wide in 1973.

About that time, the glitzy Siletz Keys project was abandoned as well, except for the few homes you now see.

Another distinctive feature of this marshland area is the proliferation of dead, gray trees to the east of the highway, which occur a little ways south of the Siletz River. They're an eerie sight, and it's actually possible you're looking at part of the process of a ghost forest in the making.

Josephine Young Park

This is one seriously hidden park, tucked away behind a neighborhood that's tucked away behind Highway 101.

Just south of the bridge after Siletz Bay Park, you're entering the final parts of Lincoln City in what is known as Cutler City. You pass the Bayhouse Restaurant and get into a quirky business neighborhood with a couple of eateries and a gallery. Take SW 62nd westward and look for the signs leading to the park. This little wayside overlooks mostly mudflats of the Siletz Bay, but parts of it are traversable. There's some dunes along the shore as well, plus picnic spots for the hungry.

Salishan – Salishan Spit

A favorite hiking spot for many and an upscale business complex are the two high-profile facets of the Salishan district.

If you're a hotel guest or a resident of the gated community, you have access to the beach from here. Otherwise, the northernmost beach access that allows you to hike the spit is down in Gleneden Beach a ways. Hiking Salishan is about an eight-mile round trip, past mostly dunes, some wildly indulgent homes and plenty of wildlife.

Immediately south of here, Gleneden Beach Loop veers off from the highway into forested business districts and neighborhoods.

Gleneden Beach

What this tiny community just south of Lincoln City lacks in size it more than makes up for in beautiful beaches. These are a curious set of beaches, too. Often, there's a rather steep slope to the tide line, which causes the waves to come in hard and noisy then stop quite quickly. It's a bit freaky at first. It feels like it's going to be dangerous, but it's not.

That is, under normal conditions. The area can get as rough, if not rougher, than other beaches because it's small and you can't away from the raging tides. Use extreme caution if tides are high or the area is rather stormy.

Also notable about these beaches are the proliferation of larger, coarser sand grains, and some tracts of blackish sands. These are always determined by the geology of the surrounding area. Just about every beach has a different composition.

The back road of Gleneden Beach Loop extends about a mile behind Highway 101, with junctions to 101 at either end. The southernmost end lies at the entrance to the State Park.

Meanwhile, some of the streets here offer hidden beach accesses. Try going west on Sijota St. until you reach Neptune St. and a hidden access there. Miles and miles of fluffy sand await you. And it's the northernmost access towards the Salishan Spit (without going through the trail reserved for guests at the hotel, that is).

If you're hiking the spit – and lucky enough to be a guest – that shaves off about 1.5 miles from your trek. Otherwise, it's much longer.

From this access, it's a three-mile hike south to Fishing Rock.

Another small access sits a few streets south near Easy St. Yes, that's its real name.

Gleneden Beach State Recreation Site

There are paved paths to the beach, a lovely lookout area above and a big parking lot – plus many civilized amenities like restrooms. It's near MP 122.

This awesome state park boasts a somewhat steep pathway heading down, which sometimes gets torn up by winter storms and then become a tad difficult to get down until state park officials have had a chance to remold the soft sandstone. The cliff walls on either side provide some stunning colors when lit by sunsets.

Heading South

Some interesting hidden parks inhabit the landscape just south of town, including the plethora of hidden little beach accesses of Lincoln Beach. Heading south, you'll find Depoe

Bay, Newport, Seal Rock, Waldport, Yachats, Cape Perpetua and the middle of the entire Oregon coast: Florence.

To find lodging in Lincoln City, Neskowin and Gleneden Beach, see the Lincoln City Lodging section. To see even more details and updated articles about Lincoln City, see the Lincoln City Virtual Tour, Maps. See the Oregon Coast Dining, Restaurant page. The virtual tour for Gleneden Beach is at Depoe Bay, Gleneden Beach Virtual Tour, Maps.

See the other books in this series on Cannon Beach and Seaside / Gearhart.

ABOUT ANDRE' GW HAGESTEDT

Andre' Hagestedt is a writer, photographer, web designer and now, by default, a videographer living in Portland, Oregon. He is publisher, editor and official web geek and marketer for Oregon Coast Beach Connection – beachconnection.net – a curious hybrid of online magazine and news publication covering travel, entertainment and science about the upper half of the Oregon coast.

Hagestedt was born in Freiburg Im Breisgau, in 1962, in what was then known as West Germany. For a brief time as a toddler, his father, mother and newborn brother lived on the south coast, but moved to the Salem / Keizer area shortly after. He grew up there, studying classical and jazz music until his early 20s, dabbling in writing on and off and eventually chasing a career in music and then photography.

By his 30s in the 1990s, his longtime hopes of becoming a rock musician failed, he began writing about rock music. Highlights included interviews with some of his heroes including Jethro Tull, members of King Crimson and Love and Rockets. He soon began branching out into other kinds of journalism, writing (or working for) a wide variety of publications, including Salem's Statesman Journal, The Oregonian, KXL radio in Portland, The Rocket, Eugene Weekly and more.

In the late '90s, Hagestedt set about documenting every single beach access on the northern half of the Oregon coast, which resulted in becoming editor of a short-lived tourism newspaper there, and eventually starting Oregon Coast Beach Connection in 2007.

Currently, Oregon Coast Beach Connection has a readership of almost two million per year and gets about six million pageviews per year.

Printed in Great Britain
by Amazon